For my girls... told you I'd do it ☺ x

Contents

Introduction:

I didn't want to write a business book

It was never my intention to pen a business book. I'd always imagined writing a novel (allegedly, we've all got one lurking inside of us). And I still aim to do that at some stage but sometimes events overtake us and priorities change. At least in the short term.

And that was kind of how this book came about. The LinkedIn 'Top Voice' award in the Marketing & Social category came unexpectedly but planted a seed of inspiration. Add that to winning LinkedIn's 'Agency Publisher of the Year' for 2015 and I realised that maybe a book explaining how that actually happened (and as I write this, I am still surprised that it did) might be a good idea. Or maybe not, dear reader, maybe not. Only you can decide that.

When I embarked upon this literary expedition, I was determined it wouldn't be a dull, dry account of my writing process. I've tried to put together some semblance of a story about why I adore writing, how I missed my vocation along the way (maybe) but through LinkedIn have reignited a desire to write more often.

Consequently, the first two chapters are more about the journey rather than the destination. If you aren't really interested in the backstory, that's ok, I totally understand. Skip those few chapters and get straight into the hints, tips and insights. I won't be offended. Probably because I will never know...

1. For the love of writing

One of my earliest, and fondest, memories is being perched on my granddad's lap in his favourite armchair, slowly reading the morning newspaper to him whilst he gently puffed away on his ebony pipe. To this day, I swear that I can still smell the fragrant aroma of ready rubbed tobacco when I turn the pages of a newspaper.

I was no more than about four years old but I can still recall being mesmerised by the words on the pages, the unusual way in which some were spelled ('chaos' springs to mind) and most importantly how keen I was to understand how they were pronounced. He would listen patiently as I sounded out any words that I didn't understand and then he would he carefully say the word to me and make me repeat it until I perfected it. Then he would lean back in his armchair, and with a knowing smile ask me if I knew what the word meant in context of the sentence which I had just read. Most of the time of course, I was clueless. And then with a quick wink (and another lazy puff on his pipe) he would explain in the simplest of terms the meaning of the word so that a small boy could easily comprehend.

As I think back, he was instrumental in developing my love of words. How they sound, how the letters are assembled, how they are used to great effect to craft a story and to engage a reader. It's an affection that I subsequently carried on into my school life and (if my memory serves me correctly) provided the first real prize in life (apart from that stolen kiss from the lovely Marion who lived at the top of Calgarth Drive... but maybe that's a story for another time).

At the age of seven I entered a writing competition at my school. The simple premise was to write a poem about the weather. Hmmm, to be honest, neither poetry nor meteorology were (or are) rich inspirational territory for me but I managed to cobble something together. I've long since forgotten the contents of the poem but I do recall my headmaster, the indomitable Mr Hindley, becoming quite animated about how accomplished it was for such a young boy to capture in writing how "dazzling glistening teardrops exploded as they ended their tumultuous journey to the ground". Or something like that. And despite the protestations of plagiarism from a few of the teaching staff (unfounded obviously) he stated his intention to enter the poem into a national poetry competition. And sadly that's as far as that went. No spectacular ending with me being hailed as the youngest ever Poet Laureate and the natural successor to John Betjeman - but it had at least instilled in me a desire to write more. And that's exactly what I did.

My next *magnum opus*? A junior competition to think up a brand new flavour for Nesquik. My concoction? A delicious blend of cassis and kumquat with a hint of juniper. Actually, that's a lie: I went for a mundane blend of 'Banana and Satsuma'. But guess what? I won. My prize? A rather nifty stunt kite, which lasted all of 5 minutes; eager to see how it performed in the gloomy northern skies of Macclesfield I dashed enthusiastically outside to road test it in rather more eager wind. It was immediately ripped from my sweaty hands. As I watched it disintegrate, swept away to oblivion over the top of the hairdressers' into the oblivion of the Weston Estate, I could only console myself with the thought that at least my words had actually won something.

So with a steely resolve to win more prizes for my writing, I set about entering more competitions - with a modicum of success. I wouldn't exactly say I was prolific but it did demonstrate a love of medium. I wanted to read and more importantly I wanted to write. And the more I wrote, the more I wanted write. My grades in English Language and Literature were always good and I was perpetually near the top of the class – if only Timothy Doggart hadn't been such a swot then I probably would have been too. Not that I'm bitter or anything.

Then at the age of thirteen, I had an epiphany. I wanted to be a journalist. Actually that's not strictly true as I really wanted to be a rock star. I wanted to be the UK's answer to Jon Bon Jovi. The problem was that if I was the answer then unfortunately nobody had ever asked the question.

Anyway my mind was made up and I immediately applied for a summer internship at the local newspaper, the Macclesfield Express Advertiser. I sent a letter written in my best script (which to be fair was, and still is, no better that the scrawl of a toddler) in iridescent royal blue ink from my beloved Parker pen (a birthday gift) and on the finest Basildon Bond (pinched from my mum's home office). I sent off the application, expecting to hear nothing back. And yet just a few weeks later I was dumbstruck when the response from the editor was to confirm a four-week stint in July of that year.

Keen to make a lasting impression, I remember turning up very early for work on the first day. Just after 8am as I recall. And as anyone who has ever worked on a local newspaper can probably attest, there was absolutely nobody there at that time on a Monday morning. The first person to arrive was the guy who ran the mailroom, who tipped up just after 9am with nothing more than a grunt and a nod for the gawky teenage in his (quite obviously) shiny new suit and shoes from Burton's.

Thankfully both the flamboyant editor and his pretty senior reporter turned up not long after in a heady haze of cigarette smoke (from him) and YSL Opium (from her). And after some brief introductions, I was set to work with some proper copywriting. Well that's if you can call the Births, Marriages & Deaths section proper copywriting. Hardly cutting edge journalism but I was grateful for what I had been given and was incredibly (I now suspect, annoyingly) enthusiastic. But it seemed to pay off because after a few days I was given something to write for the main body of the paper.

It was all fast turnaround stuff whether it was that genuine leatherette handbag being stolen from Mrs Dibble's Datsun Cherry in the supermarket car park to the rare size and interesting shape of Mr Badger's prize-winning marrows. Each day I left the office feeling that I had really achieved something tangible and was thrilled at the prospect of the good people of Macclesfield (and bordering villages) reading something that I had painstakingly written.

Consequently, you can only imagine my sheer unadulterated joy when in my final week the editor allowed me to interview a returning soldier from the Falklands War. Obviously this piece would be considerably more hard-hitting than some unusually large vegetables. I was accompanied by the senior reporter to monitor my interview technique and (I'm guessing) provide a suitable back up if my work turned out to be garbage. But all went according to plan and those 100 words or so that I managed to 'immortalise' in print on the front page, with my name attributed to them was a defining moment for me. Maybe, just maybe, this was my vocation?

But that illusion was very quickly shattered. On my final day we went to the local pub for the team to bid me farewell. *In vino veritas* as the saying goes; the senior reporter confided in me that she hated newspaper journalism because it was boring, badly paid and with limited career prospects. It burst my bubble to say the least. Particularly when the editor jumped in with both feet and confirmed all of the above whilst he tucked into his Ploughman's Lunch washed down with a pint of the landlords finest and finished off with a Benson & Hedges for dessert.

Hmm. Maybe it was time for a rethink. I was about to choose my A-levels subjects and I decided that if journalism wasn't going to be my ultimate career destination then it still had to be something associated with the written word. The answer came to me whilst studying a particular Psychology module about the Science of Communication. It covered cognitive dissonance, confirmation bias, counterfactional thinking and so on - but the component that really struck home was when we studied how advertising, marketing and branding are so powerful and the human response to this messaging whether it be visual, verbal or written. And then it suddenly occurred to me that this human element, this human reaction to messaging was what really drove my interest in writing. And, just like that, I wanted to become a copywriter.

It made my university subject choice very easy indeed: Social Psychology. My master plan was flawless. Understand about the science of communication and add that to the art of writing et voila, I could easily get myself a job as a copywriter in one of the big advertising agencies. Right? Except, there was a flaw in the plan that I hadn't thought about. I had focused almost exclusively on the theory of communication, not the practice. In a nutshell, I had no body of work. And I don't think the poem I wrote aged seven or the front page exclusive from the

Macclesfield Express Advertiser was going to impress anyone.

Yet as a naïve (i.e. dumb) 20 year old on the verge of graduating, I started to apply to some of the big guns in the ad business - J Walter Thompson, Young & Rubicam, Saatchi & Saatchi - most of whom completely ignored me. JWT sent me a courtesy letter 'suggesting' that as I didn't have a portfolio to show them, maybe I had not chosen wisely. Being a cheeky chancer, I thought I would give them a quick bell for some advice. To my surprise, someone took the call. It may have been the cleaner for all I know but her suggestion was enlightening: why not apply to be an Account Executive or maybe even a Media Planner? Now that all sounded quite promising... until I put the phone down and admitted to myself that I had no idea what either of these roles entailed.

So, given that the World Wide Web was no more than a figment of Tim Berners-Lee's vivid imagination at that time, I took myself off to the library to do some research. Neither account management nor media planning seemed particularly appealing to me (not enough writing and more of a focus on numbers from what I could gather). But if I applied for both roles then I would double my chances of acceptance and could easily swap into copywriting at a later stage. Ingenious right? As Blackadder might say, a plan so cunning that it could wear a ginger bushy tail and easily pass as a fox.

The initial phase of the plan went swimmingly well. Too well, actually. I interviewed for a role at McCann Erickson some four months before I graduated and to my utter surprise I was offered the job. The only issue was that they wanted me to start straight way. On reflection, I felt that given I had worked so hard (well at least in the final year) at university that it would be crazy to start a job before I had completed the course so I regretfully declined. But buoyed by the fact that I had managed to secure a job at the first attempt, I was confident that I could pull off the same trick twice...

And as it transpired, I could. Just a few weeks before my finals I received a letter from J Walter Thompson in Manchester. The London office had diligently passed on a copy of my CV to their northern counterparts, and I'd been offered an interview with their Media Director, the rather formidable Pauline Hackett. Well I say formidable, but her bark was definitely worse than her bite. Pauline interviewed me for one of two junior roles in either television or press. I got the latter. And so began what I thought was going to be a very short lived career in media whilst I tried to figure out how to get seconded to the creative department on the fourth floor of Astley House where I could finally begin my true vocation as a copywriter.

And almost 30 years on? I'm still trying to find my way to the elusive fourth floor...

2. How I became a 'Top Voice' on LinkedIn & 'Agency Publisher of the Year'

So, as you can see, I never made it as a copywriter. The fourth floor of that sixties high-rise building in Manchester represented everything about my dream of being a writer. The eternal symbol of what might have been. Despite trying to spend as much time as I could with cool creative types in their red-rimmed spectacles (it was the 80's), expensive sneakers and designer jeans, I was consigned to the engine room of the media department on the third floor. So close and yet so very far away.

After a few years it soon became very clear to me that because I had happened upon media as my entry point into advertising the proverbial die was cast. I was forever going to be a gorilla with a calculator. We did the numbers and they did the pretty pictures and the eloquent writing. And that was just the way it was.

I did my level best to incorporate as many elements of writing into what I did on a day-to-day basis and I guess unsurprisingly I gravitated towards media planning rather than buying. I was much more interested in the genuine insights into human nature, the media our audiences chose to consume and the products that they bought as a consequence. That has always been far more intriguing to me than shouting down the phone at someone to get a cheaper rate.

It also allowed me to focus much more on writing. There were strategies to be composed and communication plans to wax lyrical about. I poured my literary pretensions into making all those Word documents and Powerpoint presentations more interesting even if the subject matter was often a little prosaic.

I also took the opportunity to write on a fairly regular basis for the industry trade press. Back in the day I wrote for a variety of publications including *Media Week, Campaign, The Drum, Marketing* etc. on various aspects of the industry. With the advent of the internet those same articles started to appear online so naturally I set up my own blog (didn't everyone?). And I think in a way that's how I started to develop my own style (an aspect which I will examine in more detail later on in this book).

Of course not all the publications appreciated my (err, shall we say) slightly caustic / sarcastic persona. An example? Well, after a trip to South Korea several years ago I wrote an article about the really rather astounding electronic toilets they have over there. Obviously all the instructions on the control panel were in Korean but it did have tiny diagrams to provide clues about each of the various functions. My musings were built around my actual experience using ones of these contraptions. I wrote about how I pressed the button with the blue coloured 'boy' symbol on it and was greeted with a jet of warm water from the back of the bowl. However, upon pressing the pink 'girl' button (just in the spirit of scientific study you understand) I heard machinery working underneath me and looked down to see what was going on at the precise moment of squirt of tepid water sprayed right in my face. To my mind it was an amusing anecdote about life on the road in Asia. The publication I was writing for didn't see it the same way unfortunately and sent me a note saying that they didn't appreciate my (and I quote) 'flippant attitude' to my subject matter. It seems that they also failed to appreciate the title of the piece, which was 'Ah Seoul'. Seriously I don't know what their problem was - suffice to say, I didn't write for them again.

Then about five years ago I joined LinkedIn and started to post some of the articles I had written for these trade publications on the simple premise that they would reach a much broader audience. This held true, and I was always pleasantly surprised by the occasional likes, comments and shares I received.

But then, in late November of 2014, the huge catalyst for change occurred when I received a message from Andy Goldman, the Global Partner Lead for

LinkedIn. I've known Andy for a few years now and have worked with him on a number of work projects and initiatives. This note, though, was very different. It was nothing to do with work, Andy simply wanted to know why I wasn't publishing my pieces on LinkedIn.

I remember my response well. With more than a hint of incredulity (and a soupcon of sarcasm) I said that I had been publishing on LinkedIn for years. His reply was typically erudite. Of course he knew that I was reposting articles that I had written for various trade titles but he wanted to know why I hadn't tried taking the same content and putting it on LinkedIn's very own Publishing platform. To be honest, I felt more than a little bit stupid as I hadn't realised they had launched one. So with my proverbial tail now firmly between my legs, I made a commitment to give it a try.

I will be honest with you, I had very limited expectations and I shared the same with Andy. His response was simple. Just give it a go. What have you got to lose?

He made a valid point. Although I was already sharing these pieces, there was the potential to reach a new audience. I doubted it would be in the hundreds (and occasionally thousands) that I reached with my existing trade titles, but what the hell; it was worth a try.

Don't take my word for it though. In his own words, here is Andy's recollection of events:

"I remember early on, talking to Steve about publishing on LinkedIn to really define his professional profile of record. As a leader in his region and in his organisation, not to mention an industry with no shortage of competing perspectives, sharing that point of view with a broad network of like-minded professionals was a model for great amplification of both his knowledge and personal brand.

He was cautiously optimistic at first, and always questioned his approach, asking for any tips or tricks that could make his content and presentation on LinkedIn better. From the very tactical minutia of headlines, imagery and linking in his articles, to the broadly strategic themes he wrote about in advertising culture, Steve was constantly looking for feedback.

I think that thirst to develop an expertise, almost a 'muscle memory' around his voice and tone as a writer on LinkedIn was his greatest asset towards success. It remains so today. It was no surprise to me when he not only won our regional 'Agency Publisher of the Year' award, but also was named one of 10 Top Voices on the platform in 2015."

So, on January 13th 2015, I made my first ever post on LinkedIn Publishing. I had been to the Consumer Electronics Show in Las Vegas and was already committed to a review of the event with a trade magazine. That was 'genesis'. Looking back on it now,

I knew nothing about what might work (I hadn't used any pictures, I forgot to tag it) but despite that it did reasonable numbers...

<u>Leaving Las Vegas - CES 2015 Highlights</u>
(486 views, 39 Likes, 2 Comments)

The insanity of CES in Sin City is over for another year and now we are left to mull over the dazzling array of shiny kit that is about to be launched in an electrical store near you, very soon.

Was it a breakout year ? I'd say, not really. More evolution than revolution. Personalisation was a huge macro theme as was smarter, more relevant technology.

So beyond the 5 coolest bits of tech (which I reviewed in an earlier blog) what else was on offer ?

There were lots of car manufacturers this year. In fact 165,000 square feet was dedicated to them with all the main manufacturers present (which given there were none only 4 years ago, is somewhat astounding). The most incredible piece of kit was from Mercedes Benz - the F015 is a self-driving car which is basically your living room on wheels. It will never likely see the light of day as a production vehicle, but mark my words this is the future of automotive travel and we have just seen it's genesis. In terms of other car related tech, I loved the Remote Valet which is basically an enabled smartwatch / car combo that can go find a parking space after dropping you off and then return the car to you when you need it. Got to me one of those for when I'm trying to park in Vivo on a Saturday night.

As predicted in my preview of CES, the Internet of Everything was massive this year.

Beyond the smart kettle I mentioned in that post, we saw the Adidas MiCoach Smartball (a football that is packed full of sensors to measure how hard you can kick a ball, at various angles with what amount of curve etc.). I don't think Sergio Aguero needs one but us mere mortals just might. There was the slightly bizarre Edyn, which is a probe that analyses the soil in your garden and tells you what nutrients you need to add to make it more fertile. Then there was Child Angel, basically ASBO tagging for kids that are apt to wander – it is GPS / Wifi / GSM connected and so your little gems can never truly escape your clutches. And what about the Polaroid reimagined ? Then try Prynt, the iPhone case that will instantly print pictures that you have just taken. Cool huh ?

As for TV's not much to report really. They inevitably get bigger and slimmer and with even more High Definition – the 16K TV was rolled out to a slow hand clap. We haven't even got sufficient content for a 4K screen yet so why we need one with 4x the resolution is beyond me. Interfaces are getting more sophisticated and Sony launched their Android connected TV range which promises to be super smart and highly connected to all other Android enabled devices.

It was the same story with mobile phones really. Nothing truly fresh out of the box, just more sophisticated versions of bendable phones with more computing power. The only real innovation was the Worlds first holographic smartphone although I'm still trying to think of applications for it beyond a starring role in science fiction movie.

And the main highlight of CES for me ? Snoop Dogg. Not actually meeting him (though that was fun) but the fact he retweeted my DMA article about his OMG session. Pimping as Mr Dogg is apt to say. Gizoogle it. That happened. But that's Vegas for you. Baby !

So despite this fairly raw effort, it did pretty well. And I was already starting to learn some fascinating stuff. Such as the short snappy headline worked well. The main picture (me alongside Snoop Dogg – long story) certainly grabbed attention. And the LinkedIn statistics were giving me a clear indication as to where my readers were coming from. 80% of them were from either the U.S or the U.K. Given I was based in Singapore at the time, this was perplexing.

I was now hooked. And with every subsequent post I began to learn more and more about the medium. I scrutinised all the LinkedIn statistics searching for clues. I also began reading more from other writers to see what they had been writing about and to get tips on how they did it. And slowly but surely the viewing numbers started to creep up. From the hundreds in January into the thousands by March. And from the thousands into the tens of thousands by July. And eventually by December 2015 I had my first article that smashed its way past the 100,000 views mark (at the time of writing it was well past 142k and is still gaining around 100 views a day, many months after it was originally published).

And as the views began to increase, so did the number of followers I attracted. I started 2015 with less than 200 followers. By the end of the year? It was over 5000 followers. And the number is still growing.

Midway through the year, I was beginning to fully realise the impact of publishing on LinkedIn. Previously I had been somewhat dismissive of it's potential, believing that the traditional trade press I had been writing for would continue to be my mainstay with LinkedIn simply being a support. But by July 2015 I was forced to accept, through sheer weight of numbers, that LinkedIn should actually be my primary outlet.

To test the theory, I wrote an article for the online magazine Mumbrella which pitched the theory that LinkedIn would achieve a bigger audience if the same article was published simultaneously on both platforms. Can you guess which article won?

Is LinkedIn Publishing killing the Trade Press?
(836 views, 81 Likes, 10 Comments)

There has been a quiet revolution over the past 8 months since LinkedIn fully launched it's 'Publishing' service – now everyone has the opportunity to be their own author, curator and commentator without the need to have a publication validate their work. Just over 1 million individuals have now published on the platform and 45% of its readers are in the upper ranks of their industries (i.e. Managers, Directors & CEOs). Impressive stats right?

I've been writing for various trade publications for many years now and was only enticed into publishing on LinkedIn

after Andy Goldman (Global Agency Lead for LinkedIn) persuaded me to simply publish the same articles on LinkedIn. Frankly, it was nothing short of a revelation. The numbers associated with the pieces were much higher than I had initially imagined with most items racking up at least 1000 verified views. The aforementioned Mr Goldman attributes this kind of resonance to the concept of 'emotional disruption':

"LinkedIn is both a knowledge network and a personal one. As professionals define their writing voice on the platform, authentic and relevant stories are highly aspirational. When a chord is hit by an author you can identify with professionally and personally, it can be downright emotionally disruptive, cutting through the white noise of media we are all so good at filtering out"

I have also been surprised to see that the majority of my audience were not 'media' people either. Or indeed from Asia. The reality is that over 35% of the audience were from the US and in terms of industry discipline it was a fairly eclectic mix of people – anything from Finance to Farming?! But the most interesting insight was that the significant proportion were C-suite and that's an audience which (as we all know) are notoriously difficult to connect with. What's more, my number of 'followers' has escalated to almost 2500 from a base of less than 50. And if you aggregate all the views, likes, shares, tweets, retweets, comments etc. across the items I've written, the collective figure stands at over 1.2 million.

Not too shabby. Yet I would say that the most significant difference between LinkedIn and the Trade Press is the capability to make your work go viral. I wrote a piece entitled "Burn your resume – LinkedIn has made it obsolete". It did decent numbers but really took off when it was picked up by Yahoo Finance and Business Insider. Using their online trackers (where available) I've estimated that individual piece reached a combined audience of well over 150,000. A flash in the proverbial pan? Actually no. I managed to pull off the same trick with another piece entitled "Forget Greece, the real financial crisis is in China" which was featured in the Banking section of Pulse and at last count had almost 19,000 hits on LinkedIn alone.

Of course it's not just about the numbers, it also demonstrates that you don't have to be 'shackled' to write about your own industry to make a valid comment and elicit a reaction. It's really about how your work resonates with an audience and that can be measured by the 'quality' of the comments. And I have detected a distinct difference here too. The tone of voice of those comments is often much more 'professional' than those in the trade press. We have all witnessed the bile and vitriol from nameless trolls who leave their snarky comments on many of the articles published by the likes of Mumbrella. They hide behind their pathetic pseudonyms, too afraid to openly air their opinions. Come on, if you have got something to say at least have the courage of your convictions and reveal who you are. After all the author was brave enough to stand by their words, so why can't you?

Some industry observers have referenced the issue of 'content pollution' on LinkedIn and that the effectiveness of items is affected by the sheer volume of work available. I get the point but to be honest I believe that if the work is good enough then it will find its audience. It can also be aided significantly by being featured as an Editor's Pick or spotlighted in one of LinkedIn's curated Pulse sections (e.g. Technology, Social, Media etc.). I have found that when any of my items are picked up in these sections the viewing numbers are bolstered dramatically.

So does all this mean that comment from industry leaders in the Trade Press will be effectively phased out over the next few years? Well actually no I don't think that. I suggest that both platforms can co-exist in the same eco system and actually feed off each other to their mutual benefit. Case in point? I now simultaneously publish in the Trade Press and LinkedIn whilst cross-referencing both pieces to ensure that readers overtly link the two. Result? My LinkedIn viewing figures are improved by associating the piece with a credible industry publication. However, not enough industry publications follow the same logic and only use LinkedIn sparingly to promote their own content. My attitude is that they should embrace it to harness it's power.

Rather than simply push out the occasional link they should be featuring all their articles on LinkedIn as well as in their own delivery systems to maximise their potential reach. I asked Chris J Reed, CEO of Black Marketing his opinion and he was typically erudite:

"Advertising people can't advertise themselves. The media are the worst. National newspapers and trade publications from big brands like The Guardian to local ones like The Straits Times. They're just not getting it. LinkedIn has 400 million professionals on it. Do you want engage with them or ignore them? If you don't share there are more than a million people on LinkedIn publishing, often they reference trade and media sources. Work with them and you will benefit"

So Robin Hicks, for the moment I wouldn't worry too much about where you get your third party content from... but as a quick litmus test I am going to track the viewing numbers when this article and the 'mirror' LinkedIn version go simultaneously live. Let the platform battle commence!

Agency Publisher of the Year

As a fairly competitive type, I gravitate towards any form of contest so when my colleague and friend Jodi Neuhauser told me that LinkedIn had launched a race to find their inaugural 'Agency Publisher of the Year' I was definitely in.

The officially published rules were easy enough to follow...

You've got a lot to say. You have opinions, insights and advice about your industry and LinkedIn is the place to share it. Your industry peers, your colleagues, your competition and your clients are on LinkedIn consuming content every day. They could be reading your content and you could be building your reputation.

At the end of 2015, we'll be naming the Agency Publisher of the Year - one in North America, one in Europe and Middle East and one in Asia Pacific.

We'll promote the winner in the press and get their content in front of hundreds of thousands of eyeballs. Fame awaits you - all you have to do is start writing.

The only stipulation was that for each post written you had to attach #agencypublisher to the title. Then LinkedIn would use that hashtag to monitor the overall reader engagement with the article whether that be number of views, likes, comments or shares.

Now, I did consider writing more often than my usual once a week to try and bolster the numbers (I told you I was competitive) but frankly I didn't have the time to churn out much more than I was already doing. I was also concerned that maybe the quality of both thought and writing would be compromised if I tried to increase the frequency of posts. In fact, I did start some additional pieces and after a few attempts at writing something interesting I decided to jettison them. It felt like I was trying too hard to just pump out as much content as possible to boost engagement and I figured it might read that way and therefore have the opposite effect. Consequently I stuck to my principles of one piece per week and kept my fingers crossed that quality would prevail.

And so it proved to be. On the 17th December 2015, after almost 6 months of tracking, LinkedIn announced that I had won:

"Our search for the most influential voice amongst EMEA's marketing, advertising and media agencies is over – and it gives me great pleasure to announce Steve Blakeman of OMD Worldwide as LinkedIn's first ever 'Agency Publisher of the Year' in EMEA. What's even better news for our industry is that he earned the title amidst such healthy competition. We launched our Agency Publisher of the Year initiative during the summer because we knew that this was a time of seismic change for the media world – and that there was a real hunger for new thinking and ideas. We knew too that there were thought leaders out there who could provide it.

Agency Publisher of the Year was our way of bringing that supply and demand together"

James Gill

Director of Global Agency & Strategic Partnerships - LinkedIn, Europe, Middle East and Africa

LinkedIn 'Top Voices'

December 2015 turned out to be a somewhat magical month. Hot on the heels of the 'Agency Publisher of the Year' announcement came another accolade, and this one I had absolutely no idea about. When I received an email confirmation from LinkedIn senior editor Chip Cutter (yep that's a real name, not a kitchen utensil) informing me that I was one of the inaugural 'Top Voices' on LinkedIn. As I slowly read the note below I must admit that at first I was convinced it was a hoax...

"Congrats! I'm excited to share that LinkedIn's list of the best writers of 2015 is now live. We are thrilled to include you as part of it. This list celebrates the top 90 professionals publishing on LinkedIn, pulling from eight of the most engaging industries on the platform as well as LinkedIn's pool of Influencers. On behalf of the LinkedIn editorial team, congrats again!"

Was it a wind-up or could it really be true? I read it again, several times and then replied to Chip to get confirmation. Within minutes he had verified that it was *bona fide* and that I had indeed been named as a LinkedIn Top Writer.

So what exactly is a LinkedIn 'Top Voice'? Also how is it judged?

Daniel Roth, the Executive Editor at LinkedIn explained that the driving principle behind 'Top Voices' was to feature the best writers on LinkedIn so that they could highlight to readers whom they should be following or even whom they should emulate if they themselves wanted to start writing. The debut of LinkedIn Top Voices then introduced a ranked list of the Top 10 writers in eight different areas — finance, tech, marketing, healthcare, leadership, media, education, venture capital — who broke out from the crowd.

Using a combination of data and editorial signals to judge the overall winners LinkedIn also determined which writers were making a mark in their industries by measuring a host of criteria: engagement around content (especially comments, which — thanks to a lack of anonymity on LinkedIn — are unusually strong); growth of followers tied to publishing; number of times the writer had been featured in a channel in their area of expertise; and how often the contributor had been chosen as an Editors' Pick.

That last channel is vitally important and the 'Holy Grail' for anyone publishing on LinkedIn. Roth explains that it is reserved exclusively for top content that helps explain the world today; when editors select a story for Editors' Picks they are indicating that a story is worth paying attention to right now. Every single piece I write, I aspire for it to be noticed by the editors at LinkedIn. And hopefully by using the tips outlined in this book it will help you achieve just that.

Daniel Roth goes on to say:

Writing can be a lonely, nerve-wracking process: you're putting yourself and your beliefs out there for everyone to critique or build on. Those who have gotten the bug for writing know the real joy comes not in writing but in having written. Once you hit publish, the ideas bouncing around in your head turn into a worldwide conversation: You help shape the world of your readers and they help shape yours with their informed comments. As list member Marianne Griebler explained, "When someone else takes the time to thank you or scold you for the ideas you've put down in words, it's intoxicating. It's what drags us back to the keyboard again." The people on this list show what can happen when you hone your craft and develop your voice; it doesn't take being a professional writer, it takes being fearless.

I simply couldn't have put it any better.

Soon after the announcement, all of the 'Top Voices' were interviewed and a profile piece appeared on LinkedIn for each of us. I have copied mine below as, looking back on it now, this was probably the moment when the seed of an idea about writing a book about becoming a Top 10 Writer on LinkedIn was first sowed:

What he covers: "Initially I only wrote about my own industry (media, advertising and communications). After a while I began to venture into other areas of interest, from finance to psychology, and was delighted by the response. And my tone of voice? Pretty much always tongue in cheek."

Favorite post: Me, My Selfie & Die

Why he likes it: "The danger associated with taking a selfie is now such an issue that the Russian government has launched an awareness initiative to prevent more carnage. Such as 'don't take a selfie with a loaded gun.' Seriously, you can't make this stuff up. It wasn't the most successful item I've written in terms of numbers, but given the fantastic comments I received, it really brightened up the days of a few readers and I love that."

Not on his LinkedIn profile: "I secretly wanted to be a copywriter but couldn't get a job. So I went into media with JWT thinking I could swap within a few months. That was almost 30 years ago. And I'm still in media."

As you will notice, several of the themes captured in this short interview are explored in more detail throughout this book and I guess that's because it was where that aforementioned 'seed' went from being sowed to germinating. Am I take this seed analogy too far now? Yeah ok, I know. I'll stop.

3. Top 10 Tips on becoming a Top 10 Writer on LinkedIn

No false modesty here, I nearly burst with pride for a few weeks in December after the two announcements were made by LinkedIn and it left me with a healthy warm glow for the duration of Christmas. Or maybe that was just the mulled wine.

When the yuletide festivities were over, the prospect of the New Year looming and with the euphoria beginning to wane (just a tad) I finally asked myself a pertinent question. *"How the hell did I manage to achieve that?* And I wasn't the only one asking that same question.

It seemed to be all the more unbelievable when I started to consider the facts. The numbers pretty much speak for themselves. LinkedIn currently has well over 410 million registered users. Those who are publishing on a regular basis number over 1 million and this figure is rising rapidly. These writers are pumping out around 150,000 articles every single week. Over a year, that's almost 8 million articles or reviews. As you can probably imagine, simply trying to stand out in this veritable tsunami of words is really rather tough.

So how had I done it? No one had told me how to achieve it. It had also never been an aspiration – I had no idea that either 'Top Voices' or 'Agency Publisher of the Year' existed when I first started to write on the platform.

Was there a 'secret sauce' to success? Had I stumbled across a formula without even realising it? The more I asked these questions, the more intrigued I became. And it soon dawned on me that although there was no 'silver bullet' when it came to capturing the attention of readers there were certain tricks that I had inadvertently picked up along the way. I had often surveyed the detailed stats that LinkedIn supply to their publishers for clues. I played around with subject matter, titles and tone of voice. And that is what I am keen to share with you so that you can ensure that your very own *magnum opus* is read ahead of the other 149,999 items published in the same week.

So here we go, I'm putting everything I have learned as a 'Top Voice' and 'Agency Publisher of the Year' out there to help you find your voice. All the hints, tips and insights that I can think of have been included. I have held nothing back in my pursuit to get other like-minded individuals with a passion for the written word to start publishing on a regular basis.

Where possible, I have also tried to illustrate these tips with examples from my own LinkedIn portfolio. Oh and if you like what you read then don't forget to take a look at all my latest posts (cheap plug) and become a follower (even cheaper plug).

So here we go, let's begin with my very own Top 10 Tips on how to bolster your chances of becoming a Top 10 Writer on LinkedIn…

Writers Write

My favourite author is Stephen King. Maybe not a conventional choice given he has been largely dismissed (unfairly in my humble opinion) as an author of shock horror novels. *Carrie, The Shining, Christine, Needful Things, It, The Dead Zone* etc. But you may be surprised to know that he also wrote the prison drama *The Green Mile*, the coming of age saga *Stand by Me* and the epic tale of escape that is *The Shawshank Redemption*. Commercially he has always been a phenomenal success but critically he is not well loved by the cognoscenti. I think he has largely been misjudged as a writer. I believe he is a master storyteller who, in the years to come, will be held in the same high regard as the likes of Charles Dickens, Bram Stoker and Arthur Conan Doyle.

Consequently, I am a huge fan of the book he wrote about his craft called *'On Writing'*. It's a book that was almost never written. The true story is that King was knocked-down by a drunk driver whilst out walking in 1999. He was almost killed and spent several months in hospital and convalescing at home. Fearing that he had lost the ability to write following the accident he decided to resurrect a manuscript that he had begun a few years earlier about his love of writing. In a way the effect was cathartic. It reminded him about the passion and desire he had for the medium and it actually reignited his writing ability. Just think, if he hadn't done so then we wouldn't have witnessed such modern classics as *Under the Dome*.

In the book, King talks about a number of facets that have made him such a prolific writer. One of the main reasons is that he simply adores writing. In his words? Writers write. And so do I. Pretty much every day, even if it's only for five minutes before boarding a plane, sat in the back of a taxi or maybe even on the toilet (full disclosure, don't judge, you know you've done emails on the throne so why not a LinkedIn post?).

When I started posting articles on LinkedIn, I decided to heed the advice of Mr King and I opted to write at least one piece per week. Minimum. No matter how busy I was at work, or whatever commitments I had with the family, even if I was on holiday, I would write an article each and every week. I felt that was achievable, even if I wrote for just ten minutes a day.

And the point is that I didn't try to find the time. If you try to find the time then you will inevitably fail. If it's something that you genuinely want to attain, you have to make the time. My inspiration? None other than Barack Obama and the attitude he has towards physical fitness. To be fair he is a pretty busy guy. Arguably, much busier than you and I. Put together. But he makes time to exercise every single day because it is important to him (this theme also became the inspiration for an article I wrote, as you will read later). So if writing is salient to you, then you will make the time to do it. Won't you?

"Writers write" isn't exactly rocket science but I like to think it's profound in its obviousness. If you are going to be a writer you obviously need to write but I would warrant that a lot of people talk about being a writer without often putting pen to paper (or, more likely these days, keyboard to cursor to screen). Writing, like so many things in life improves with practice - the more you do it, the better you become.

For me writing is fairly painless, as we established in the first chapter of this book. I cherish the process so it comes relatively easily to me. But I totally concede that it can be quite intimidating for many people. My advice is relatively simple. Don't publish immediately. Write a few articles before you make your first post just to get you into the swing of things. Play around with your subject matter and vocabulary. Try to figure out what appeals to you and also try to develop a way of writing that you feel is distinctive, or at least reflective of some aspect of your personality.

Once you have written a few articles and are reasonably happy with them, it's time to take the plunge and bounce them off a few friends / colleagues. Ask them specifically for their comments. Listen to their viewpoints, both positive and negative (don't be discouraged if they are hyper critical – trust me, when you do start publishing you will get criticism from your readers so be prepared to develop a thick skin). Try to be rational and objective. Where you feel they have a valid point, incorporate their suggestions into a revised version of the same piece. Then run it past them again as a final sense check.

The following piece is a strong example of that. I wrote this item about Maria Sharapova failing a drugs test and the fact that her key sponsors were swift to drop her. I wanted to get the piece out quickly to benefit from the interest surrounding the news so I wrote it in an airport lounge in about 30 minutes. To be honest, the initial version didn't really have a hook and probably wouldn't have been that successful if I hadn't sent it to a friend for his opinion just before I caught my flight. It proved to be a valuable few hours as he pushed me to find an angle. After a rapid rethink, I reworked the article to consider that sponsors had become more risk averse over the past few years after the high-profile cases of Tiger Woods, Lance Armstrong and Oscar Pistorius...

Just (Don't) Do It... are Maria Sharapova's sponsors too quick to ditch her?

(14,467 Views, 716 Likes, 169 Comments)

Tennis superstar Sharapova has flunked a drugs test and been suspended from the sport. That's astounding in itself but the alacrity with which key sponsors such as Nike, Porsche and Tag Heuer have abandoned her is also quite astonishing...

So firstly, what is the background? Yesterday the five-time Grand Slam champion attended a personal press conference at a Los Angeles

hotel with the industry predicting that she was about retire at the tender age of 28. As it transpires she had set up the meeting to confess that she had been caught using a banned substance by the World Anti Doping Agency (which I guess effectively means she was announcing her retirement anyway).

The tests, taken at the Australian Open in Melbourne a few months ago, proved that she had taken Mildronate (or Meldonium) which has been prohibited in all professional sports since 1st January 2016. The drug is capable of significantly enhancing physical performance and endurance. As such it has been likened to the blood-boosting substance EPO, made infamous by shamed celebrity cycling 'juicer' Lance Armstrong.

By Sharapova's own admission she has been taking the drug for the best part of a decade to treat 'diabetes' (which is rather odd given that it's a drug prescribed for heart conditions) and had simply continued it's usage without being aware of the consequences of its relatively new outlawed status.

So that's the back story but you can read more about that pretty much anywhere on that interweb thingy right now. What I'm more fascinated by is the way in which several of her key sponsors have rapidly deserted the top earning female star like rats leaving the proverbial sinking ship. Literally within hours of the announcement, Nike ditched the Russian sports idol from her most lucrative contract. She had signed an initial 8 year deal with them (extended in 2010) for a cool $70million which also included her very own range of sports apparel.

Within rapid succession Swiss luxury watch manufacturer TAG Heuer and prestige German car marque Porsche followed suit.

According to Forbes she earns around $30million a year in endorsements which also include American Express, Avon and Evian. So far these sponsors are not commenting upon the situation.

So why are some of these brands so quick to ditch their stars when the going gets tough? I believe the key reason is down to three high profile sporting superstar scandals of the past 7 years, which have got progressively more serious as each one has occurred.

Back in 2009 we had the lurid 'tabloid' stories of golf legend Tiger Woods being exposed as a serial philanderer. Despite several brands deciding to jettison Woods as soon as the story broke, Nike took the brave decision to stand by their man.Alan Ferguson, MD of marketing consultancy The Sports Business claimed that Nike's:

"whole golf proposition was built around him. They had spent millions of dollars and simply couldn't afford to drop him"

Or maybe because his impropriety wasn't deemed serious enough? That particular kind of 'cheating' may be considered immoral but isn't directly connected to his sporting prowess.

Next up? The aforementioned Tour de France drugs cheat, Lance Armstrong. Nike stood steadfastly by their iconic brand spokesman for many years despite constant allegations of him being an EPO drug cheat. When the truth finally came out, Nike admitted that they had been "misled" by Armstrong for the best part of 10 years and dropped him like a hot stone.

And most recently, the ultimate ignominy of Paralympic champion Oscar Pistorius who murdered his girlfriend in a hail of bullets on

St Valentines Day 2011. As soon as the news broke his sponsors (including Nike, Thierry Mugler and Oakley) were quick to distance themselves from the South African 'Blade Runner'.Nigel Currie, ex-director of sports marketing agency Brand Rapport and now head of NC Partnership put it most succinctly:

"This is very different to the Tiger Woods and Lance Armstrong cases; this is life and death. There's no coming back from this"

So given these three sensational / high profile cases, it really doesn't come as a huge surprise to me that brands are being more swift and decisive in their crisis management. Sharapova has clearly transgressed and publicly acknowledged the situation for what it is. Despite offering some (rather implausible) mitigating circumstances, she has admitted to taking the banned drug and has accepted liability in the matter - Just

(Don't) Do it. That said, she is now effectively 'damaged goods' and it's clear that major brands don't want any part of that negative association.

So to answer the initial premise of this piece, I don't believe that her sponsors have acted rashly. Given the circumstances, they have simply acted swiftly and sensibly. What do you think? Were her sponsors right to drop her immediately or should they have waited for the results of the upcoming inquiry?

The article certainly caused some controversy and the opinions were somewhat polarised. There were a fair amount of haters who were clearly Sharapova supporters and felt she had been unfairly judged. To be honest, it was great for the viewing figures and that wouldn't have occurred if I hadn't asked for the opinion of a colleague.

By adopting this approach you will get into the habit of polishing the pieces that you write before you publish, a tactic that I will explore in more detail in chapter 3.

Does all this seem a little bit too much like hard work? Well if it does, it's because it is. No escaping the truth that writing takes time, patience and a modicum of skill. And you have to enjoy doing it. If you don't enjoy doing it then frankly there isn't much point continuing. If you don't get a kick out of writing, the humble reader will spot it a mile off.

Be Authentic

In 2013, the Boston Consulting Group conducted a survey with 2,500 U.S based consumers and found that authenticity was one of the main qualities that attracted them to a brand, particularly for Millennials, who want to have an "engaging, authentic" relationship with them. And I believe the same is true for readers on LinkedIn. They are attracted to reading your piece because it reflects the way you think and it resonates with like-minded individuals.

My best example? Well I guess that's best epitomised by my best-read piece which was published in December 2015. With my exaggerated use of the word best, you might think it's my best work? In my opinion it isn't, but who am I to judge? The readers do that for you:

6 Stupid Office Rules That Should Be Banned

Rules in the workplace. Without them we'd have anarchy right? Or would we? According to an article by Dr Travis Bradbury in the Huffington Post most companies fall into the trap of instigating several morale sapping rules for every employee based upon the inconsiderate actions of a small minority of transgressors. Hardly seems fair does it? So Dr Bradbury has outlined nine dumb directives and I have featured my top six...

Banning use of social platforms - now I think we would all accept the need to restrict access to some of the more (shall we say) 'unsavoury' sites available on the internet but why do some companies insist upon stopping access to the likes of LinkedIn, Facebook and Tumblr? The commonly held belief is that social media stifles efficiency but there is a counter-argument that these platforms are incredibly useful tools in the work environment - for example scoping someone's profile whilst checking them out as a potential employee or downloading an image for a presentation. And anyway, we are resourceful beasts and if our access is blocked at work we will inevitably utilise our trusty smartphones as the interface instead.

<u>Totally inflexible working hours</u> - In my recent article '*Working 9 to 5 is no way to make a living*' I wrote about why Netflix and Virgin have dispensed with the traditional 9 to 5 working practice and introduced fully flexible working hours and vacations. As Sir Richard Branson puts it:

"the focus should be on how much people get done rather than how much time they spend on it"

So if that's the case then why do some companies and/or bosses insist upon totally rigid working hours? Dr B talks about the injustice of being pilloried for turning up to work 5 minutes late despite the fact that you regularly work evenings, weekends and even on vacation. He goes on to say:

"if you have employees who will fake a death to miss a day's work, what does that say about your company?"

<u>Excruciating E-mail Policies</u> - now personally I've not come across this particular imposition but seemingly some companies are starting to introduce software that prevents employees sending emails unless it falls into a pre-approved list of topics. Travis and I agree that this is simply a matter of 'trust' - again I mentioned this in my 9 to 5 piece where I quoted senior analyst Sam Stern from Forrester Research on the matter:

"if you trust and empower people and give them a chance to rise to the higher expectations, the vast majority of people are able to do it"

To be honest, why would you even bother hiring someone if you don't trust them especially for sending something as basic as an email?

<u>Stopping the use of Smartphones</u> - a clear cut example of the original premise of this piece, where the inconsiderate actions of the few adversely affect the majority. Just because a few chatty Cathy's and blabbering Bobs can't stay off their phones for more than five minutes doesn't mean that the rest of us should have to suffer.

But to be frank, we all have lives outside of the workplace and there is the occasional need to be in contact with the outside world either through a call or some kind of messaging. Whether it's a poorly child or that the pesky dog has escaped from the back yard again, companies need to accept that life goes on beyond the working day and a diligent employee will always make up the time (and be incredibly grateful that you cut them some slack).

<u>Draconian Dress Codes</u> - who should decide what is appropriate to wear at work? Here is a concept, I say the individual should choose their attire. Again it's simply matter of trust (and I suppose, to a certain extent, taste). I think I know what to wear for each occasion. I don't see why wearing jeans and a t-shirt is an issue (although admittedly, as I work in the media industry I would concede that it's maybe a little more accepting than say banking). I may not be the epitome of sartorial elegance but dressing down doesn't make me any less productive. Actually I

believe that because I'm more relaxed, it's going to accelerate my productivity. The point is that we should embrace self-expression. Hmmm, well at least to an extent...

<u>'One size fits all' Performance Evaluations</u> - suffice to say we all excel at different things and have unique personality traits. So then why do so many companies assume we are all identical and evaluate their employees using a pre-determined set of criteria?

According to the HuffPo article, by incorrectly evaluating people's performance it will just make employees feel like a 'number' and reinforce any insecurities they have about being fired for not having the attributes that they believe the company is seeking.
So there you have my top 6 but which annoying office ordinances do you despise?

When I have written articles which are reporting the news (like a review of the 'Consumer Electronics Show' or a list of movies that are being released that year), the response has always been relatively weak – views are often just in the hundreds rather than the thousands.

On the flip side, the most popular items that I have written on LinkedIn are the ones where I have taken a particular stance on a subject. I will be honest, I am more than happy to put my opinion out there to be challenged and never expect everyone to agree with me. Okay so I lied a little bit there. I actually prefer it when readers agree with me but I don't mind it (too much) when they don't. I kind of adopt the principles of Pareto's Law (on the basis that the 80% will side with me, of course).

At least proffering a point of view is generating some kind of debate or discussion, which is always healthy. What I don't do is write something that I don't believe in just to stimulate a war of words. I fundamentally have to be convinced by what I am writing about. If it is my informed opinion and I have put the effort into researching it then I am willing to steadfastly protect my point of view if the need arises.

And that extends to the comments, likes and shares too. If people have taken their valuable time to make a comment on one of my articles then I will always try my best to answer them. If it's a simple congratulatory message then I probably wont get time to write a thank you for every single one but I will at least click 'like'. For the more interesting or challenging comments then I will almost certainly leave a comment - and yes, that definitely includes the negative ones too.

It's important not to come across as being unprofessional, hypercritical or argumentative in your reply. Keep it respectful and measured at all times. Don't forget this is LinkedIn not Facebook or Twitter. I always thank the commenter for their opinion and for taking the time out to post their viewpoint. I will then outline my counterpoint or validation and leave it at that. If provoked further, I usually extinguish further comments by simply agreeing to disagree and leave it at that.

Have a Unique Style

Your tone of voice is your signature. Without it you simply become another writer on LinkedIn. I have had some astounding comments from the people who follow me on a regular basis (which, as I mentioned earlier, has escalated to over 5000 since I started writing on LinkedIn). All writers love their readers. It's validation for what they do. So when I get comments about my writing style from my readers then I really take it on board.

Interestingly it seems that the majority of those readers tend to pick up on the same thing. No matter what I write or when I write it, I always have my proverbial tongue stuck firmly in my (also proverbial) cheek. Even when the subject is quite serious, such as the article I wrote about the financial crisis in China then I still try to find some jocularity in the story:

Forget Greece, the real financial crisis is happening in China

Whilst the World watches the Greek tragedy of its imploding economy, over in China there is a far more significant drama unfolding. Since mid-June share prices on the China CSI300 have plummeted by around 30%. In real terms that equates to approximately $3.2 trillion dollars which has been wiped off their stock market.

Trying to put that number into context is rather difficult (how many zeros in a trillion again?) but here goes... as a yard stick it is actually higher than the United Kingdom's GDP was in 2013 (a rather modest $2.7 trillion). Scarier still, it completely dwarfs the estimated $380 billion debt in Greece... don't forget (as if you could) that there are 1000 billions in a trillion.

What is also intriguing and yet equally alarming is that this dramatic drop came on the back of several months of solid growth. Since November 2014 Chinese stocks had more than doubled and this was largely driven by relatively small investors. The BBC estimates that between 80% to 85% of buyers are the so-called 'Mum & Dad' retail investors playing the stock markets and, for the most part, using borrowed money.

Only last year, the Chinese government were actively encouraging these small investors to start buying more stocks in a concerted effort to accelerate the market. And initially that plan appeared to have paid off. However, some experts are now claiming that the policy has ultimately backfired due to the 'herd mentality' of these small investors – basically if their friends and family start selling then they will do the same and a domino effect occurs with everyone selling at the same time.

The effect? Panic. The result? A crash.

In some quarters, comparisons are already being made to the infamous Wall Street Crash in 1929 which heralded the start of the biggest ever economic catastrophe in the US which ultimately led to the Great Depression. Decisive steps are being taken by the China government to halt the decline and almost half of Chinese company shares have been temporarily suspended. But according to CNN the market is still expected to slide much further (predicted to be as much as 8%) in the early days trading next week. Du Changchun, a senior analyst at Northeast Securities said: *"I've never seen this kind of slump before. I don't think anyone has. Liquidity is totally depleted"*

Of course there is a flip side to all this doom mongering. There are plenty of industry pundits who argue that because China is still essentially a centrally-controlled economy it often defies the usual conventions of economics. They predict that even if the stock market does continue to crash, the impact will be no worse than in 2007-08, when the Shanghai Composite fell by two-thirds. Yet after a massive fiscal and monetary stimulus by the government, the broader economy effectively didn't miss a beat.

On measure though, the naysayers appear to be winning the debate epitomised by a live prediction tracker on the Telegraph website where 60% are predicting a calamitous meltdown for the Chinese economy and only 40% claiming it is no more than a proverbial storm in a (China) teacup…

As an additional example, I have republished another piece that I wrote in September 2015 about the alarming increase in deaths caused by people taking 'selfies' and some of the measures that governments

have taken to prevent more incidents. I think the title
kind of sums up my style quite succinctly...

Me, My Selfie and Die
(3,191 Views, 179 Likes, 36 Comments)

**Dying to take a selfie? Think again, it may be
more dangerous than you imagine. True fact?
More people have been killed taking selfies
this year than in shark attacks. *Mashable*
have validated the numbers and 12 people
have died this year taking selfies compared to
8 deaths by shark attack. So why is this
seemingly safe pastime so perilous?
With an estimated 1 million selfies being
taken each day I suppose it isn't a huge
surprise that the number of associated
incidents is rapidly on the rise. The number 1
reason why people shrug off their mortal coil
whilst taking a selfie? Falling. Only last week a
Japanese tourist died when he fell down some**

stairs while attempting to take a selfie at the Taj Mahal.

Next up? Being hit by some form of moving vehicle. Back in April Peruvian Jared Frank became an overnight sensation on YouTube when he attempted to take a selfie in front of a moving train and ended up being kicked in the head by the conductor.

And I guess this is exemplifies the point because people are taking ever increasing risks to capture the most extreme selfies. It appears that idiocy has no boundaries as there are literally thousands of snaps portraying people perched on top of the Worlds highest buildings, running away from the bulls in Pamplona or even attempting to catch a selfie with venomous snakes. Yep you read that right. In July, *CNN* reported the story of a certain Mr Todd Fassler from San Diego who was bitten several times whilst trying to take a selfie with a rattlesnake. The result? He lost part of his hand and was landed with a medical bill of over $150,000. There are no words...

Meanwhile, over in Russia, the government have realised that careless selfie taking is becoming a genuine risk to it's citizens (honestly, you can't make this stuff up). *CNET* reported that Russia's Ministry of the Interior held a press conference a few months ago to launch a novel safety initiative prompted by over 100 serious injuries and 10 deaths in the last year. These include a guy who shot himself whilst posing with a pistol and another who took a picture whilst grabbing an exposed wire to see what would happen. Funnily enough he was electrocuted. In an effort to assist some of the more (er) 'challenged' members of society the Russian government have introduced a rather nifty

chart outlining the types of selfie one should avoid...

Handy tips include avoiding taking selfies in front of moving trains, on the back of speedboats, in front of tigers, with a loaded gun or whilst trying to fix your TV aerial. Clearly all sound advice but they still missed out trying to take a selfie with a rattlesnake.

The kind of comments I received are indicative of the type of followers I tend to attract. Ones with a slightly dark humour given their reactions:

"Thin the herd of narcissists"

"Hahahaha! No, I know I shouldn't laugh. It really is appalling! Thanks Steve"

"Couldn't help but chuckle at some of these - Darwinism 101"

I guess the point here though is that I always write for myself, not the reader. If you find it amusing then there should be someone else out there who shares the same sense of humour.

So what am I suggesting here? Should you adopt the same facetious style as yours truly? Nope, that's not what I am saying, unless you have the same acerbic sense of humour as myself. What I am maintaining here is that whatever style you choose you ensure that it reflects some aspect of your personality (remember that earlier point about authenticity?). And then hope there are a few more readers out there who share the same traits.

Step out of your Comfort Zone

Of course it's always easier to 'play it safe' and stick to your own industry or sphere of knowledge. But follow the line of least resistance and you will most likely fail. What is much more challenging, interesting and rewarding is when you choose to write about something that you are much less familiar with.

My writing habits have morphed dramatically over the last year of writing and the subject matter I choose has increasingly eclectic. I was used to writing articles for the media, advertising and communications industry because I've been doing that for at least 25 years now. But, to be honest, that's a relatively limited audience. And I have also figured out that it's actually not the only thing I am interested in. I may not profess to be an expert in some of the other subjects that I write about (and some might say I'm not an expert in my chosen field either) but that doesn't stop me having a valid opinion does it?

So over the past year I have explored some of my other interests. And when I have branched out into other fields such as finance, human resources or psychology the appeal of the piece has broadened and it has resonated with a much more diverse audience.

And frankly, this approach has worked by securing more engagement in terms of views, likes, comments and shares. For example, I wrote a post about how 'sarcasm' is used in the work environment and whether or not it is appropriate - the response I achieved was phenomenal and came from a wide spectrum of careerists ranging from acting to zoology. Seriously? Well take a look for yourself why don't you?

Sarcastic = Smarter. Seriously?
(24,883 Views, 1,310 Likes, 166 Comments)

Sarcasm, according to the old adage, is the lowest form of wit. Well not according to a recent study in *Psychology Today* which

claims that being a sharp tongued wise ass proves you are smarter than the average bear. But be warned, use it too much and you may damage your career prospects…

The ability to insult stupid people without them realising it has long been a mainstay of business community communication. You don't say. It's also used to great effect in a slightly different form - something my U.S based friends call a 'roasting' (which means something very different in other parts of the World, but I digress). From what I understand of the phenomenon, this is a verbal volley of 'good-natured' jokes aimed at an individual and all at their expense. Sounds absolutely charming.

It seems that the reason why sarcasm is so successful in the workplace is because it is often associated with high intelligence. A study by the *University of Haifa* demonstrated that the ability to understand sarcasm depends on a carefully orchestrated sequence of complex cognitive skills in specific parts of the brain. Dr Shamay-Tsoory, the psychologist leading the study, said: *"Sarcasm is related to our ability to understand other people's mental state. It's not just a linguistic form, it's also related to social cognition"*

Part of the reason for the claim of elevated intellect is that the brain is effectively being exercised more when one is being snarky as opposed to when someone is making a sincere statement. Scientists have proven the theory by monitoring the electrical activity of the brain and found that the grey matter of a smart aleck works considerably harder when the subject is being sarcastic and even more so when trying to decipher it.

Richard Chin of *Smithsonian Magazine* describes it as "mental gymnastics". Sarcastic, satirical or ironic statements all force the brain to think beyond the literal meaning of the words and understand that the speaker may mean something entirely different:

"Just like training your muscles, if you do 50 push-ups a day, over time, your arms are bound to be toned. So sarcasm, as a form of 'mental exercise' functions the same way. Over time the extra work leaves our brains toned too"

So should we all turn up to work tomorrow and start being super sardonic with all our work chums? I'd be rather inclined to say no. It seems that any use of sarcasm at work must be used somewhat sparingly unless you want to be labelled a smug, superior smarty pants. So 4 top tips have been kindly provided by the 'experts' to ensure your wisecracking doesn't cut too deeply:

- Know your audience - that doesn't just mean you have to understand them, it literally means make sure you know them before you test out your acerbic jibes (unless you like being slapped)
- Scan before you send - generally don't send anything facetious in an email or text. For some reason these forms of communication are most often taken literally, not laterally. If you absolutely must, then use a smiley face to make sure the person gets the point you are joking. Unless you are being ironic, then maybe use the emoticon with a wink?
- Examine your motivations - why do you want to be acidulous? Is it because you have some self-image issues? Feelings of inadequacy versus the recipient of your verbal joust? If you feel uncomfortable

with who you are maybe you shouldn't use sarcasm. You saddo ;)

- **Err on the side of caution - if you feel your stinger might cause any real offence to the person it's aimed at or even the people around you, then simply cease and desist**

To conclude, if you believe that sarcasm makes you smarter, use it judiciously as it can cause much more harm than good. After all there is a clue in the title. The derivation of the word sarcasm comes from the Greek phrase *sarkazein*. Its meaning? To tear off the flesh like dogs. Enough said.

Get Inspired by Reading

I am a firm believer that reading is just as important as the writing itself. And I am a voracious reader. I look for inspiration in everything I read each and every day. As the aforementioned Mr Stephen King puts it:

"If you don't have time to read, you don't have the time (or the tools) to write"

I use a variety of primary sources but my daily mainstays are LinkedIn Pulse (naturally), Huffington Post and Mashable. That said, inspiration can come from anywhere and content has caught my eye in a dazzling array of places including in-flight magazines, a CNN news report, a random tweet or a post on Facebook. In terms of subject matter, don't restrict yourself. If it is something that appeals to you and you think you can find an angle, then go for it. I have written some fairly diverse commentaries on everything from the Banksy 'Dismaland' art exhibition in the UK to the growing phenomenon of Adult Colouring Books:

Adult colouring books are not just child's play
(873 Views, 128 Likes, 16 Comments)

So what's the hottest book trend in 30 years? Steamy '50 Shades of Grey' style cable-tie action? Nope. Salacious Hollywood gossip pulp fiction? Nah. It's colouring books for grown-ups seeking an analogue release to their daily digital lives (who knew right?). And with sales up almost 2000% this year it's no wonder that titles like *'Secret Garden'* currently represent half of the Amazon top 10 bestseller list.

Arts and crafts have long been used as a way to unwind, but why all of a sudden have colouring books taken off and become such big business? (and it really is big business too with Johanna Basford the 'ink evangelist' behind the aforementioned *'Secret Garden'* shifting over 3.5 million units in the past 2 years). The most popular belief is that people are becoming tired of constant online access, either through work or their social lives, and are seeking some respite with a desire (if not a need) to unplug. Author Matt Cain explained his freshly acquired love of the medium in an article for the Guardian:

"If I switch off the phone, computer and TV and concentrate solely on choosing the right shade of blue, avoiding going over the lines and slowly filling up my page with colour, all my other concerns, I've discovered, fade to nothing"

The therapeutic effects derived from indulging in some form of artistry are well documented and resonate with people of all ages. Art therapist Susanne Fincher, has published several colouring books and claims that the simple pastime can lift a persons mood, reduce their anxiety and relieve stress. Well, I guess it's a lot more relaxing than blowing the head off another flesh eating zombie with an AK47 in the latest (re)incarnation of Resident Evil.

Anyhoo, Ms Fincher goes on to say:

"Art making is a powerful intervention. Neuroscientific research has shown that through the use of art therapy, the human brain can physically change, grow, and rejuvenate."

So have these 'colourists' (as they have been termed) completely abandoned the digital platforms that they have become so weary of? Actually it seems not. An item in *The New Yorker* claims that once they have completed colouring-in their pretty pictures they proudly take a snap of their masterpiece and upload it onto the likes of *Facebook* and *Pinterest*. Hmm, given that they turned to colouring books to escape the clutches of their 'evil' technology doesn't that rather defeat the object?

Anyway, to be honest, I'm not quite sure about the stress relieving powers of this publishing phenomenon. In the spirit of science (or should that be art?) I attempted one of these cutesy stress beaters. Unfortunately I got wound up like a Swiss watch when I discovered that I simply couldn't keep my rudimentary pencilling neatly between the lines. Bah. It seems that my school art teacher was probably right all along, despite my protestations to the contrary, when she informed me that my self-portrait resembled a King Edward potato...

So maybe colouring books are not really my thing. Consequently, I've decided that I am going to wait until next year when I'm rather hoping that a publisher launches some dot-to-dot books for us ageing folk. Or maybe even some adult pop-ups? (although lord knows what the subject matter might be about).

I suppose it's little bit like the writing itself in so far as you need to read everyday. Focus on your favourites by all means but don't be a slave to them. Variety, after all, is the spice of life (as they say). Try to mix it up every once in a while. Read something fresh to seek some inspiration. You never know where your next article is coming from.

Size is Everything

Who says that size matters? Well actually I do. When it comes to writing an article on LinkedIn size is crucial. In this instance, trust me, less is more. As much as you might wish to write your equivalent of 'War & Peace' on the internal workings of the modern day common rail diesel engine it is pretty unlikely to get any kind of traction with a sizeable audience (if that is your aim). If you are only targeting a very niche audience and want to convey a quality message to this limited group then that's absolutely fine. But I'm guessing that if you are reading this book then you want to maximise your audience as much as possible so I suggest you keep it brief.

There are no hard and fast rules when it comes to the length of your literary piece but as a quick rule of thumb I always aim to keep my articles to less than a 5 minute read. Ideally even less. You have to accept that your audience are busy people. In the main, they're probably working and reading in their spare time either commuting, during a break, at lunch or before they go to sleep. So anything too long and turgid is going to get them rapidly switching to an alternative item.

One of the techniques I have employed is the use of the '2 Minute Skinny' – basically the lowdown on a subject which guarantees a limited amount of time to read the piece. I have done this on several occasions, whether it be the launch of the Apple Watch or a quick review of an event such as SXSW:

<u>Missed SXSW? Read the 2 minute 'skinny' here...</u>
(497 views, 19 Likes, 4 Comments)

Didn't make it to Austin TX for SXSW '15? Want to know what went on across the 800+ sessions? Take a 2 minute time-out to read about the 5 key talking points and maybe even impress your boss with a well chosen soundbite:

Future of travel - from alternatively fuelled vehicles to revolutionary car sharing options and from self-driving cars to flying vehicles. Yes the Jetsons-style flying car is coming to you by 2017 according to its makers Aeromobil. And apparently there will be a driverless version just a few years later...

Haptics – now there is a new one for you (don't forget, you heard it here first). Derived from the Greek word for 'touch' in this context it basically means some form of tactical tactile response to a technology (try saying that quickly). For example, the *Pavlok* app and associated wristband will punish its user if they do something bad (eg. like smoke, overeat etc.) by giving them an electric shock. Or a slightly more positive approach is that of the *Alert Shirt* developed by Foxtel in Australia which uses wearable technology to let football fans experience the body blows taken by their chosen player during a game.

Convergence Programming - the barriers that have traditionally separated the music, film, sport and interactive industries are rapidly evaporating. This was a theme we saw at CES in January best epitomised by the Omnicom Media Group session featuring Pepsico, Snoop Dogg and Revolt. There was a whole day given over to it here and the highlight (for me at least) were the *mi:mu Gloves* which are a wearable tech for aspiring musicians who can't play an instrument (like me). Become Eddie Van Halen in an instant. Without the skill. Or the guitar...

Accelerator - not exactly new (now in its 7th year at SXSW) but still managing to pull in the crowds and genuinely excite the people who participate. Selected start-ups present their ideas to a packed auditorium and panel of judges. The 'most innovative' award went to BioBots who manufacture human-tissue via 3-D printers (yuck), whilst the overall winner was Slantrange whose drone systems enable crop farmers to survey large fields for problems such as pest infestations.

Agencies & clients killing the cool factor – for a decade SXSW has largely been considered the cooler cousin to CES. This year though, some have argued that SXSW had sold out to the corporate big boys. There was barely an event which hadn't been sponsored in some way. The core mission of the event when it launched in 1987 was to find new bands. Now it's grown exponentially and become something far beyond that original musical remit. Less like Austin, more like Vegas. No opportunity was missed including a plane flying a Grumpy Cat flag courtesy of Friskies. Yep, that happened. Dave Rosner (Head of Marketing at ZEFR) said "SXSW has become a

must-stop-by versus a cool-stop-by. Critical but certainly no longer 'emerging." Which is all good but, on the flip side, people are already touting the likes of C2 in Montreal or Dmexco in Cologne as potential heirs to the geek tech throne.

A short, sharp, selective summary that makes the most of the sound bite. It may not have garnered the most views I have ever received but I didn't expect it to. It's a quick hit, will likely last no more than a day or so but it serves its purpose.

Write for Yourself

When mere mortals publish their work on LinkedIn they are not doing it for monetary gain or stardom. Artists, musicians, sports people and thespians are often the same. They do what they do because they love it. If fame and fortune follow it's unlikely that they will spurn it (who would?) but it probably wasn't the key reason for driving them to do it in the first place.

Writing on LinkedIn doesn't earn you any money either. Trust me, writing this book won't make me a millionaire. Except maybe in lira. For those of us who do it, it's because we enjoy it. And that makes you free to write about whatever the hell you want. If you write for money that makes matters a whole lot more complicated because then you are then being paid to do a job. And that means, potentially, that you lose the element of control by being forced to write what someone else wants you to write.

What you can consider though is writing to elicit a response. Actually that can be a phenomenal way to hone your skills. Over time, you can find out what your audience really wants to read and figure out ways that you can provide it. It can help you make a living out of your writing. But don't concern yourself with any of that until you learned how to write for yourself.

The next example is a decent demonstration of that. As you may have noticed, I have always had a keen interest in psychology and am fascinated by those dynamics in the workplace. I'm intrigued by how many people see themselves as 'wage slaves' and become thoroughly miserable in their chosen careers. However they find it almost impossible to break out of that mental fugue to help themselves. My intention is to write a book on the topic at some stage and this piece is a precursor to that:

Are YOU making yourself unhappy at work?

According to a recent Gallup Poll up to 18% of us are unhappy with our jobs. And given that psychologists know that unhappiness leads to serious health issues, maybe we should do something about it? Particularly when, according to Dr Travis Bradbury most of the fault lies not with your job but with yourself...

Now, the more cynical amongst you might be thinking that the simple solution to contentedness is all down to one thing. Money. That's the reason why we work in the first place right? But actually it seems that cash isn't the key determinant to contentment. Research from the University of Illinois states that people who earn more moolah are only marginally happier than their less fortunate compatriots. And that even includes the uber wealthy who earn more than $10 million per annum.

So what does determine whether you are joyful? Well, another study conducted by the University of California indicates that a complex mix of life circumstances and genetics accounts for about 50% of a person's happiness. The remaining half? Apparently that is entirely up to you.

Now there is relatively little you can do about life circumstances and absolutely nothing you can do about genetics. But you can change your outlook on life and in a Forbes article by Margie Warrell she delves into that very subject. She postulates that you have the capacity to change 3 things:

- Change *what* you do (e.g. if your job makes you miserable then do your best to find another one in a company or industry that you prefer)

- Change *how* you do it – adopt new habits, ways of doing things and try to pursue a more positive frame of mind
- Change *nothing* – continue to be a miserable old bugger and continue complaining about how life has dealt you a bad hand

As you might expect neither Margie, Dr B, nor I recommend the final option.

It may not be practical to change 'what' you do right now - you can't simply switch companies or (even more problematic) convert to an entirely different career. We all have bills to pay so maybe the more pragmatic option (in the short term at least) is to reorient 'how' you do your job in a more positive (maybe even realistic) manner?

Thankfully, Dr Travis offers up some practical ways of doing just that and I have listed (and cheekily renamed) my 7 favourites below:

The Future Fibber – how many times has your annoying inner voice told you that everything is going to be just fine when... 'I get a promotion' or when 'I get a pay rise' or when 'my boss gets hit by a bus' etc. ad infinitum, ad nauseam. Come on are only fooling yourself. None of these things is going to make you happy. Well they might do for a short while but that initial buzz of Bob being flattened by a double decker will quickly dissipate. Then you feel remorse and the dawning realisation that you now have his job to do as well as your own. Anyway the point is that you need to focus on what makes you happy in the 'here and now' not on something that may (or may not) happen in the future.

The Materialist - this is a remnant of the Boomer and Gen X generations who have always been obsessed with acquiring material possessions. Bigger house, better car, new kitchen, expensive watch etc. There are 2 points to make here. Firstly, there is a mountain of research that proves beyond doubt that chasing possessions is ultimately unrewarding. Actually they can add to your unhappiness because when you finally attain them you get that cold hard realisation that it didn't make you as happy as you expected and that in turn makes you feel unhappier. Secondly, Millennials (thankfully) have an entirely different outlook. They crave 'experiences' instead of 'things' - activities and passions that they can share with family and friends, which in turn makes them significantly happier.

The Victim Mentality – "it's not my fault and there is absolutely nothing I can do about it" –

we all know people who operate from the default position that someone up there just doesn't like them. Dr Bradbury says that the key flaw with standpoint is that it...

"fosters a feeling of helplessness, and people who feel helpless aren't likely to take action to make things better. While everyone is certainly entitled to feel down every once in a while, it's important to recognise when you're letting this affect your outlook on life"

Bad things happen to good people all the time but the reality is that everyone has at least a modicum of control on how they control their lives for the future as long as the individual is at least willing to try and take action.

The Eternal Pessimist - the self-fulfilling prophecy of pessimism. Basically if you expect things to go badly, chances are that they will. Not only that, but people avoid pessimists. Frankly they are just not that much fun to be around are they? I used to work with a colleague whose glass was never even half empty. His always contained the dregs. Even when we won a huge piece of new business and we were cracking open the Veuve Cliquot he was bemoaning the fact that we were going to be hugely busy because we didn't have enough resource to service the business. Seriously, get a grip. Things are rarely ever as bad as they may seem.

The Constant Complainer- complaining is a closely linked companion to it's buddy pessimism. Often seen together curmudgeonly discussing how atrocious things are and by doing so simply reaffirming all those negative beliefs. Although talking about what bothers you can be cathartic you need to strike a balance between it being therapeutic and adding more fuel to your unhappy fire.

The Rug Sweeper - when you take responsibility for your actions you will be a far happier soul. Miserable people though are threatened by the mistakes they make and consequently try to bury them away. These 'skeletons in the closet' rarely disappear, they lay lurking in the shadows waiting to jump out and scare the living daylights out of you when you least expect it

The Green Eyed Monster - if you find yourself constantly comparing yourself with others, then it's time to start appreciating what you have and stop coveting. Cutting down on your Facebook time might help a little...

So there you have it, if you are feeling fed up at work give these handy tips a try. And, go on, give us a smile :)

The Power of the Edit

"Kill your darlings, kill your darlings, even when it breaks your egocentric little scribbler's heart, kill your darlings."

Again I'm shamelessly quoting my literary idol Stephen King from his book 'On Writing'. His advice on editing is, in my opinion, a prerequisite to effective writing.

The main problem with most writers is their singular lack of ability when it comes to editing their own work. And I am as guilty as most. When I have written a piece, particularly when that piece hasn't been born easily and I have grafted away at it for hours the last thing I want to do is start 'killing my darlings' as soon as I have written it.

But sadly, most of the time that is precisely what you need to do. I have only ever written one piece that I haven't needed to edit. Or maybe I should have edited it but didn't have the time. It was an off-the-cuff piece about Uber and why their so-called rewards programme is so terrible. I had just taken an Uber to the airport and I had realised how much I am now spending with them these days. The same is true of SPG Hotels but their loyalty scheme is amazing and it encourages me to use them all the more. But Uber? Frankly I get pretty much... nothing. Nada. Zip.

Uber, why is your rewards program so rubbish?

(1,552 Views, 116 Likes, 15 Comments)

I love Uber. Great app, swift service, swish cars etc. And that's why I use it. A lot. And because I use it all the time, it got me wondering about their loyalty scheme. Which, unlike it's service, turns out to be uber-crap.

They do have a loyalty scheme but for some strange reason they don't talk about it (maybe because it's so poor?). It is entitled 'UberVIP'

and becomes available after you have taken 100 Uber rides. Your account will be automatically upgraded and you will see a 'VIP' option miraculously appear in your Uber app alongside UberBlack, UberX and UberTaxi. That is if you are in one of the very few cities that its available, which, as far as I can gather is limited to New York, Washington and Denver. Seriously, just 3 cities? And all in North America?

So if you are 'lucky' enough to be in one these cities, what benefits can you hope to glean from your hard earned VIP status? Well, prepare to be hugely underwhelmed. You are guaranteed a driver with a 4.8+ status (ooh I hear you gasp). And what else? Well you get a (and I quote) *"high quality car"* (I know, I know, you can barely contain yourself right?). And the 'coup de grace' ? It's the same pricing as UberBlack. And that, dear readers, is it.

I'm sorry but that's not exactly the kind of caché a loyal user would expect.

Interestingly though, they do partner with some of World's leaders in loyalty. For example, you can link your Uber account with your Starwood Hotels SPG account and accrue an SPG point on your account for every dollar you spend (although given that you need about 10,000 points for a stay at a decent hotel then spending $10,000 on taxi rides to get a free nights stay doesn't seem to such a great return on your investment).

They also have arrangements with American Express (who know a thing or two about loyalty schemes) whereby you can earn 2x AMEX points whenever you ride and also Capital One who offer a 20% cash back if you pay for Uber using their card.

So come on Uber, wise up. Learn a little from your smarter partners and get serious about

your loyalty program before some of your dedicated users decide to take their business to the likes of Lyft with the lure of free wi-fi and maybe even the occasional free ride...

Anyway, I digress. The point is, I wanted to get something written whilst it was fresh in my mind and so I wrote the item in less than 30 minutes in the lounge at the airport. With nothing more than a quick check for spelling and grammar, I hit the publish button and promptly boarded the plane. And instantly regretted it. Because if there is one thing I have learned from writing on LinkedIn, it's that you should never publish your first draft (that said, the Uber article did pretty well so maybe I shouldn't always be so cautious and be a little more spontaneous).

I have found that the best writing I have done (in my own opinion at least) comes when you have given your pieces a little time to settle. It's what bakers call proving; a rest period to allow the dough to rise. And, in a similar kind of way, that is what I try to do before I finally publish an article. I will often write the piece over two or three days, letting it rest for while and then working on it again. Going over what I have already written, amending where necessary, adding to it if needs be and then leaving it again for another few hours or even a day or two.

And even when I have completed this process of proving and the piece is finished I will almost always walk away from it again before a final edit the day that I publish (sometimes that process takes considerably longer too as you will read on in the book).

What's more I will always ask someone to read it before its published. Just as a sense check more than anything. I've even been known to get my children to read my work. I figure that if they can get something from it then anyone can. I don't pretend that my work is highbrow or worthy, but I would like to think that it's accessible so the perspective of a child is actually perfect.

I've also taken my own advice when it comes to the editing of this book. It's easy to become a little 'word blind' when writing an extensive narrative and reading your own work over and over again isn't easy as you rapidly lose perspective. After at least a dozen personal edits and reworks, I handed over the final draft to a talented young editor, Jordan Harries, who works for the Financial Times.

I'm grateful for her keen attention to detail and the way she has helped me to refine and polish the content. Helping me cut out what didn't fit, enhancing the salient points and drawing attention to places where the reader should focus proved to be invaluable. And it also reminded me that a fresh pair of eyes on my weekly LinkedIn posts is always worth seeking out.

Spelling, Grammar and Punctuation

If there is one way to murder and article, then it is poor spelling. Once misspelled word undermines the rest of the piece and ultimately makes the reader switch to something else. I know that it's the same for me too. Even if the content of the piece is exceptional, it only takes one word to be spelled incorrectly for me to decide that it wasn't worth reading in the first place.

Back in the days of paper and ink, one could be forgiven for the occasional errant word. Writers were reliant upon their knowledge of the English language and hopefully a broad vocabulary. If all else failed then a decent dictionary and a thesaurus would be trusty aids. Time consuming to use but equally necessary. These days, with the advent of ever increasingly sophisticated desktop publishing options there is little excuse for making spelling mistakes. Your little electronic friend will be kind enough to point out your errors with a brightly coloured squiggly line. Not only that, it will also go to the trouble of providing you with a vast array of synonyms if you select the appropriate option.

Where possible I always try to write my pieces in Word first rather than straight into the LinkedIn template. Not only does it allow you to play around with the content much more but it also takes out that element of risk of clicking that publish button inadvertently.

Now obviously, we all make mistakes and sometimes we miss our friendly electronic suggestions as well. We have all done it but the great thing about the publishing platform on LinkedIn is that you can always go back into the item once it has been published, edit the mistake and hopefully no-one is the wiser (apart from the first movers who spotted the error and take great delight in letting you know about your faux pas).

And please don't use made up words ('irregardless' is one of my pet hates) unless you specifically want to make up words to prove a point, as I did in this piece from November 2015:

7 words you say that can harm your career (1,967 Views, 63 Likes, 18 Comments)

Business Insider have just highlighted 6 words (+1 added by me) that you should avoid to make you sound smarter at work. Given we should eliminate these words from our vocabulary, I have also suggested 7 new ones to replace them...

Firstly let's take a look at the words we must eradicate:

1. *Stuff* - the rationale for dispensing with 'stuff' is that it doesn't really mean anything. Or possibly worse, it could mean everything. Or nothing.

2. *Maybe* - the epitome of 'wishy-washy.' As we all know ambiguity is always perceived negatively. Well definitely maybe...

3. *Honestly* - by inserting this randomly into a sentence, it kind of implies that you are telling the truth about that particular point but lying about pretty much everything else

4. *Really* - It was really great. Really? Yes really. Oh really. Annoying isn't it? And really (really) adds no value.

5. *Amazing* - when something is amazing, it is genuinely exceptional. Love is amazing. Your new shoes are not. Consequently when you use 'amazing' all the time you diminish its power.

6. *Never* - never say never again. It's too definitive. And it's also likely to be a lie as you probably would do it (whatever it is you say you would never do) given the right incentive.

I'd also like to add my own contribution to make it 7. And that word is 'like'. I don't like, like. Particularly when it's used as a comparison.... *"it's like, you know, like it was honestly the most amazing stuff like, you know, really really like something I've never seen, like, ever before. "*

Like, you get the point right? So I say, like, stop saying like. Makes you sound dumb. Like.

Now then, if we are to dispense with some words in our business lexicon, I think it's only fair to replace them with some new words. Just to even things up right? Given that it's rather difficult to randomly make up entirely new words (trust me I've tried and it all sounds like Klingon) I'm attracted to the trend for 'blending' two existing words to explain something that was previously difficult to categorise. Here are 7 examples of my current favourites:

1. *Nonversation* - (n) a completely pointless conversation with no purpose often heard at

the start of conference calls. Basically the modern day equivalent of small talk

2. *Askhole* - (n) someone who asks completely pointless questions in a meeting just so that their voice can be heard (read my previous article Shut Up!)

3. *Cellfish* - (n) those people in meetings / presentations who inconsiderately focus on their mobile phone screens rather than concentrating on what is being discussed

4. *Unkeyboardinated* - (adj) those moments when you repeatedly make mistakes when trying to correct something on Powerpoint or Word (which usually occurs when your colleagues are watching over your shoulder)

5. *Textpectation* - (n) the overwhelming anticipation one feels when waiting eagerly for a text, email, Whatsapp message from a colleague or friend

6. *Beerboarding* - (v) the act of taking a colleague out for several drinks after work with the express intention of getting them

tipsy so that they pass on gossip or office secrets

7. **Nerdjacking** - (v) - filling a conversation with totally unrelated material (e.g. a hobby) simply because you know something about it and the other (often disinterested) person doesn't

So what are your pet hate words in business? And have you got any new blended words to add to my list?

So we've established that there isn't much of an excuse for making a spelling error these days. What is a tad more difficult is grammar. Now, I have always been reasonably good at spelling but my grammar hasn't always been the best. It has been a long time since I took my English Language & Literature exams and I think it's fair to say that my grammar and punctuation skills have become somewhat rusty (what's the betting that I have made some grammatical howlers in this very book? – evens I'd say).

As my editor has pointed out on several occasions (much to my chagrin) I have an annoying (her word not mine) habit of putting adverbs before verbs. "Gently puffing on his pipe" as opposed to "puffing gently on his pipe". I think it's just because I tend to write like I speak and it's a hard habit to break. So I decided not to bother making all the amends she suggested...

Thankfully we are helped by the same electronic aids that assist us with our spelling. That said, I haven't found them to be quite as accurate and the alternatives that are suggested often just don't make any sense. Some of the most common mistakes that I see can be easily avoided. For instance their (to indicate possession), they're (a contraction of 'they are') and there (when referring to a location).

Or what about the use of it's and its? Well it's is short for it is and its just isn't (or is not).

Then there is your and you're. If you're meaning to say "you are," the correct word is "you're" (just as I did to start this sentence) otherwise the word is "your."

And then there are those irksome commas and where to use them. Simple rule? Slow down when you're writing and read your copy out loud. When you feel there is a need to pause, insert a comma. You don't want to make this mistake: "Let's eat, children" as opposed to "let's eat children. An important distinction to make I would suggest.

These are just a few of the common mistakes that people make and I could go on listing them for ages. But this isn't a book about perfect grammar, so we should press on. What I will say is that you really should check both your spelling and grammar as many times and in as many ways as possible. Use the electronic aids to help you, read your piece through as many times as you can and, if possible, get someone to proof-read the final draft. Spelling and grammar mistakes can be very costly when it comes to maintaining a readership so be sure to invest some quality time in avoiding them.

Think Ahead

As I made a commitment to write at least one article a week (and, to date, I haven't shirked that once) I am writing a considerable amount over the course of a year. To be constantly inspired takes a lot of inspiration! Of course, regular reading (as I have already outlined) is often the key.

However, there are occasions when you can't quite find a topic that really floats your boat. Inspiration tends to be a little like that, does it not? Feast or famine.

So, over time, I have collected certain ideas and topics to be utilised at a later date just in case I head into a fallow period for free thinking. At any one juncture, I probably have at least three and up to seven different 'projects' that I have given working titles and collected reference sources for. Quite often, I will have a near-complete article that simply needs a modicum of finessing to make it come alive. And then there are the abandoned pieces. My island of misfit toys. A ragbag of thoughts, musings and ideas that are in desperate need of some serious re-engineering to give them some semblance of a decent article.

It's an adroit way of ensuring that you regularly have something to fall back on in those lean periods where there is nothing rousing in the news and you've plainly run out of ideas.

Now you may think that these would be the ones that don't work as well when they are eventually published. On the contrary, they often tend to do quite well. Maybe it's because they have been given time to mature like a fine wine. Or possibly because they have more attention is lavished upon them over a longer span of time which means they are better thought through. It could be all of the above. Or none of them. What I'm trying to say is that you shouldn't give up on an idea just because it didn't work out the first time around. And this next example is a quite exquisite example of that. Firstly because it was one of those 'sleepers' that had lain neglected for many months because I couldn't find a way to make it work until I saw a quite brilliant quote by Thomas Edison which reignited my passion in the long-forgotten piece. And in addition, Edison's core theme of unswerving perseverance in the face of adversity was a fitting match for the subject matter of the article:

Why Failure is the key to Success
(16,254 views, 1,783 Likes, 180 Comments)

In the movie Apollo 13, the NASA flight director is famously quoted as saying *"failure is not an option"*. Well in business there are so many variables at play that it more or less guarantees that failure isn't just an option at some stage, it's pretty much a certainty. And yet it's one of those truly annoying idioms which gets blurted out with alarming regularity.

LinkedIn is awash with articles and lists of how to be successful in business, but there is very little written about why falling flat on your ass can be a good thing. According to a recent article in *Entrepreneur*, we all need to start acting like scientists. To a boffin, failure is just another data point which will ultimately lead to the right solution, or as the author of the piece puts it:

"For the scientist, a negative result is not an indication that they are a bad scientist. In fact, it's quite the opposite. Proving a hypothesis wrong is often just as useful as proving it right because you learned something along the way"

There is a school of thought (which I subscribe to) that people who enter into a project with a fear of failure are actually more likely to do so because their negative mind-set will affect the outcome. Firstly, you are closed off to creativity because anything innovative automatically carries a higher element of risk. If it hasn't been done before then it is, by its very nature, unproven and hence is more likely to go belly up. And secondly, if you do try something unique and it initially fails you are more likely to give up rather than try again and realise the full potential of the idea.

The real trick here is to teach yourself to accept failure, learn from it and move on. Dr. John C. Maxwell is a World expert on leadership and his key insight is very simple. It's all down to perseverance. He cites the example of Thomas Edison who was apparently asked, whilst developing the prototype for the light bulb, how he could keep going after continued failure. His reply?

"I have not failed. I've just found 10,000 ways that won't work"

But it's not just the likes of Edison who failed spectacularly at some stage in their career. The history books are littered with examples of frustrating foundering. Walt Disney (lost his first job for being a 'dreamer'), Abraham Lincoln (one of four US Presidents who went bankrupt) and Henry Ford (burned though his initial investment without producing a single car) are just a few notable examples.

Yet each and every one of them remained resilient and adhered to the 5 golden rules of making failure work in your favour:

1. Reject Rejection - achievers know their self-worth and never consider themselves a failure even when things don't play out the way they wanted

2. Take Blame - never inculpate others, accept the situation for what it is, suck it up and set about making it right

3. Failure is Temporary - a huge chasm from which you can never get out or a stepping

stone to something greater? Guess which route winners choose?

4. **Realistic Expectations** - we all fail from time to time. Nothing and no-one is perfect. Accept it

5. **Focus on Strengths / Diminish Weaknesses** - recognise your talents, focus on them and if you have flaws then try and work with people who can make up for your shortcomings

Let's be honest, we've all been there at some stage. That hideous moment when something goes wrong and you simply want the ground to swallow you up. After almost 30 years in business I've lost track of the times that I have cocked up (although I'm sure there are a few people out there who might like to remind me!). But the ones who go on to win are the ones who pick themselves up off the ground, dust themselves down and simply carry on. Or as Sir Richard Branson puts it:

"I will work day and night to avoid failure, but if I can't, I'll pick myself up the next day. The most important thing for entrepreneurs is not to be put off by failure"

So when and how have you screwed up and what did you do to get back on track?

As you can see, the viewership was actually really high and the shares and comments were almost exclusively positive (for a change). They included a note from a university graduate from the U.S who had read the article on her way to a job interview. It seems she had quoted a few lines from the piece in response to a question about how she deals with failure in the workplace. I never did find out if she managed to secure the role or not but the fact that she was so grateful for what I had written and used the piece as inspiration to try and secure her first ever job simply fills me with joy.

4. The rules of 'Engagement'

So now you have my Top 10 tips on how to create engaging content on LinkedIn. Hopefully you will have determined your style of writing, you will be able to portray your voice in a way which will attract readers and your subject matter will be astounding.

That isn't the end of it though. Actually you have only just begun. Having fantastic writing isn't sufficient to get people reading. Don't forget you are competing with those other 149,999 articles published in the same week. I hate to admit it but great content is only the beginning, now you have to market it in the best possible way.

Having being involved in advertising, marketing and communication for some time I have picked up a few tricks along the way in terms of branding etc. To be entirely honest though, the majority of tips I have picked up on LinkedIn have often been through trial and error, spotting a trend in my analytics interface or by simply copying the strategies of others who are attracting an audience much bigger than my own — there is no shame in that, imitation is the sincerest form of flattery right?

Using a Snappy Headline

I'm estimating that something like nine out of ten headlines I read on LinkedIn are terminally dull. The bad ones pretty much fall into three categories.

Firstly, just plain boring. Who, for example, is going to read an article entitled 'The Basics' (a real headline). The basics of what exactly? Origami? Sky-diving? Jumping through hoops of fire attached to zip wire? Actually any of these would have been way more exciting than the reality, which was something to do with the stock market (to be honest I can't really remember too much about it as I was falling asleep after the first sentence). Maybe it should have been called 'The basics – for curing insomnia'. At least it would have been more honest and realistic.

Then we have the headlines that are too long:

"POLITICO Playbook: 1 YEAR to INAUGURATION DAY -- CLINTON ALLIES PLAN NEW ATTACK ON SANDERS: He's a little nutty!"

Actually I have a feeling that this particular headline could quite easily fall into the following 'incomprehensible' category as well. Look I'm sure it means something to someone (even if it's only just the writer) but if you want to entice someone into reading your work of genius then it's a good idea to create a dash of anticipation with a headline that might actually have a fighting chance of engaging them.

Finally, there is the simply incomprehensible. "The Swarming Nano-Agents of Algorithmic Cognition". I kid you not, that is an actual headline. At first I thought it might be the latest instalment in the Transformers movie franchise but alas it was not. I have absolutely no idea what it means (and that's after reading the article as well). The point here is that to broaden the appeal of anything you write then it absolutely must have a headline that has a chance of connecting with them. The subject matter may be complex and it may be difficult to lure readers but by using the simple literary technique of an eye-catching headline will not detract from the purpose of the piece. I'm not talking about dumbing down here either – there is a big difference between simplified and simplistic.

So what happens when you get the headline right? Well, it has a dual effect. Initially it attracts the attention of prospective readers, as I have already argued. But if it is eye-popping enough to catch the attention of one of the editors at LinkedIn, then you stand a far better chance (assuming that the article is as good as the headline) of getting them to feature the piece in Pulse or one of their curated sections.

Whenever I have managed to get one of my items featured in any of these sections, it has led to a huge increase in traffic. On average, I have found that the pieces that have been picked up by the various editors at LinkedIn have delivered an audience four times as large as those articles that weren't featured. And occasionally the audience for a featured piece has been up to ten times as big.

So how about comparing some headlines that did work with a few that didn't?

Well to spare the blushes of any other writers on LinkedIn, I have decided to feature only my own work. First up, an example of a strong headline (which was hopefully backed up by a strong narrative). Published in December 2015, this was about the fully flexible working hours introduced by the likes of Netflix and how it is a more realistic working practice that the traditional 9 to 5 model. So, I simply took the title of the 1980 hit single from Country music star Dolly Parton, tweaked it slightly for my purposes, et voila, it got picked up by the editors and was featured in no less than three sections (Recruiting & Hiring, Millennials and

Operations). It also went into my Top 10 most viewed articles I have published on LinkedIn:

Working 9 to 5 is 'no way' to make a living!

(6,323 views, 430 Likes, 42 Comments)

In the immortal words of Dolly Parton *"working 9 to 5 what a way to make a living... it's all taking and no giving".* **Well that is unless you work for Netflix who have dispensed with the traditional 9 to 5 working practice and introduced fully flexible working hours and vacations. A sensational initiative or simply a 'House of Cards' ? See what I did there? ;) Oh please yourself then...**

The battle for the best millennial talent is constantly raging and employers are progressively cognisant of the desire from prospective employees to offer creative compensation packages, more

absorbing work environments and flexible working hours. The guys at Netflix are pretty much the pioneers of this practice. When they started in 2004 they soon realised that their traditional 9 to 5 working policy wasn't, err, working for them.

So they took an incredibly brave step and introduced what they call their *'freedom and responsibility culture'*. Simply stated, they scrapped their policy of fixed working hours / holiday allocations and replaced it with a, erm, no-policy. In other words, staff could take time off whenever they wished and for as long as they wanted. There was no need to ask for any approval and time sheets were eliminated. The employees themselves were the only ones to decide if they fancied a few hours off each day, take a week off on a whim or even a month if the urge compelled them. No rules. Netflix based their no-policy strategy upon one solitary factor. <u>Trust</u>. Now there's a concept, trusting the people you have employed...

Basically they decided to trust their own people to determine when they would take a break. As long as the individual felt entirely reassured that their absence would not be detrimental to their colleagues, clients, the company or their careers they were entitled to take off as much time as they jolly well pleased.

Totally preposterous right?

Wrong. The scheme has been a resounding success. In an article by Huffington Post they have cited it as one of the pivotal reasons for the stratospheric success of Netflix and quoted senior analyst Sam Stern from Forrester Research on the matter:

"if you trust and empower people and give them a chance to rise to the higher expectations, the vast majority of people are able to do it"

Netflix is always eager to extol the virtues of their stratagem but are equally keen to add that it only works because it hires "fully formed adults". The company then simply treats them as such by offering almost unlimited freedom to "take risks and innovate" without being constrained by complex layers of process.

But surely this maverick approach is just a one-off? Well, actually, no it isn't. Inspired by the innovative proposition, Sir Richard Branson introduced a very similar scheme for Virgin staff in 2012. According to Branson the less rigid attitude towards working hours has been enabled by increasingly sophisticated technology which effectively means people can work pretty much anytime and anywhere:

"the Netflix initiative had been driven by a growing groundswell of employees asking about how their new technology-controlled time on the job (working at all kinds of hours at home and/or everywhere they receive a business text or email) could be reconciled with the company's old-fashioned time-off policy"

According to Branson, the key to its success is a simple matter of quality versus quantity:

"the focus should be on how much people get done rather than how much time they spend on it"

So that's it then. Every company should introduce flexible working for their employees and trust them not to abuse the privilege. Case closed, article over.

Well, in the spirit of balance, maybe it's not as clear cut as it first appears... There have been a few cases where a more 'enlightened' management approach to flexibility hasn't always paid off... In 2013 Marissa Mayer, CEO at Yahoo! made the startling decision to rescind their 'work from home' policy on the basis that it's *"not what's right for Yahoo right now"*. The message that was being telegraphed by Mayer? Come in to the office where we can see what you are doing. Oh and you better look busy.

And, whilst the (supposedly) altruistic approach offered by Netflix provides some astounding incentives don't be fooled into believing it's just a haven for slackers. The Netflix culture is one that is driven solely by success. They don't demand their proverbial 'pound of flesh' in terms of time spent working but they absolutely insist upon results. In fairness to Netflix they make it abundantly clear what is required of their employees in their much vaunted Culture Deck:

"Sustained B-level performance, despite 'A for effort', generates a generous severance package, with respect."

Zero ambiguity there then. Hard working losers can leave.

So what do you think? Is the 9 to 5 really a thing of the past? Is the prospect of fully flexible working hours something that would appeal to you in your chosen industry? Is it just a cynical way of making you work harder but without the invisible barrier of time constraints? Or as Dolly herself might say "It's all right, but it's all wrong".

This piece benefitted immensely from a headline that really resonated, and developed into a successful piece in terms of views, likes, comments and shares.

Sadly though, not all of my musings have fared quite so well. Now, I could moan about my resolute belief that people just didn't understand my 'art', or that it was ahead of its time or a million other excuses. The harsh reality is that the title didn't draw them in.

The story in itself was really quite interesting. A cute, tweeting, hitchhiker robot traveling around the globe with the assistance of humankind. Unfortunately the social experiment didn't have a happy ending. The robot met a sad demise in Philadelphia after being found decapitated in a ditch.

It should have been a great feature, with a strong social commentary and a few gags thrown in for good measure. After my usual editing and checking procedure I had high hopes for how it might fare. But I was wrong. It struggled to break over 200 views and had very few likes / comments / shares. Why? Well it's difficult to precisely determine what went wrong but on reflection I'm sure that my choice of headline was a huge mistake. I chose to use another song title. Although this time not from the country & western icon that is Dolly Parton but rather the obscure 1970's US soft rock outfit Styx. Not only that but I picked a song from their (even more obscure) rock opera era (Spinal Tap anyone?) as the basis for my headline.

Now there was me thinking how very clever I was but was rapidly brought crashing back down to earth by almost everyone I asked about it. After I had published it of course (always get people to proof-read it before, remember?). Not one of my friends or colleagues had ever heard of the song (or the band for that matter) and hence the (so-called) humour was entirely lost on them.

It's like telling a joke that only you laugh at. As it happens, that's something I am also very familiar with, courtesy of my kids...

Domo Arigato, Mr Roboto...

The Terminator movies would have you believe that humankind should be very afraid of robots. But given the sad demise of *hitchBOT*, found beheaded and decapitated in a Philadelphia ditch this week, maybe robots should be more scared of us...

hitchBOT was a social experiment of sorts, the brainchild of Toronto's Ryerson University. The initial premise was very simple. *hitchBOT* would tour the world using the generosity of mankind. It couldn't move around independently and hence needed a helping hand from the carbon based lifeforms that inhabit this planet. Although hitchBOT was festooned with a dazzling array of electronic wizardry including GPS, a high resolution digital camera, the ability to post on Twitter / Facebook and with a built-in voice decoder / recorder, the rest of the machine was distinctly low tech - his body was merely a bucket, his head was a cake saver, he had garden glove hands and wellies for feet. Purposely cute I guess, to encourage people to take him on his expedition.

And initially the friendly hitchhiking robot did rather well. It made it all the way across Germany, the Netherlands and Canada with barely a scratch. Its odyssey was tracked enthusiastically by kids and geeks across the globe who were enthralled by its epic journey which included bizarre appearances at a glitzy wedding and a comic book convention. Unfortunately though, his trek across the U.S was somewhat short lived. Despite a promising start attending a baseball game at Fenway Park in Boston and being photographed in Times Square New York, *hitchBOT* met his untimely demise in

Philadelphia (the ironically named City of Brotherly Love) last weekend. Dismembered, decapitated and dumped in a ditch. Domo arigato Mr Roboto (sorry - I couldn't resist squeezing in a quick Styx classic).

And then, as if to add insult to injury, some (so called) pranksters claimed to have security camera footage of the moment that *hitchBOT* shrugged off his 'electric' coil. But it transpires that two local Philly vloggers had actually faked the video to encourage further social discussion on whether the 'death' of *hitchBOT* was an act of simple vandalism or an expression of Robotophobia. Either way it's clear that bad things happen to good robots.

There are various campaigns underway to resurrect the unfortunate android. The City of Philadelphia (unsurprisingly) has lead the way with offers from various tech companies to raise *hitchBOT,* Lazarus-like from the dead. At the same time a Kickstarter campaign has been started to crowdsource funding to rebuild it. Hmm. Somehow I cant help thinking of the opening sequence to that classic 70's show the *The Six Million Dollar Man...*

"We can rebuild it. We have the technology. We have the capability to make the world's first bionic hitchhiking robot.
hitchBOT willbe just that. Much more than it was before. Better. Stronger. Faster"

Though maybe next time with a titanium exoskeleton and some form of weaponry system? Either way one thing is for sure... *hitchBOT,* just like *The Terminator...* will be back.

The moral of this section is that you need to think long and hard about the headline for your piece.

An ex-colleague of mine, Ian Gee from Geenius Consulting, always used an acronym for these occasions: KISS. I know it sounds like a reference to yet another 70's rock band (you'd think I'd learn given how badly the Styx reference went down) but it's not actually a reference to Messrs Simmons & Stanley from the face painted rockers. In this context it means Keep It Simple, Stupid.

Try and ensure that your title is short, to-the-point and intriguing enough to make the reader want to know more. My advice is to write the article first and then figure out the headline later. Hopefully you will have a flash on inspiration as you pen the piece and a good title will more or less write itself.

Choosing an Engaging Picture

A picture, as the saying goes, speaks a thousand words. And as much as a killer headline will draw in the punters, a well-chosen picture to highlight your piece will have exactly the same effect. Combining the potent power of them both is the dream ticket and is your best guarantee of decent viewership. Double whammy.

The brain processes visual imagery 60,000 times faster than it does text so it makes sense to incorporate some stimulating pictures into the piece to signpost or complement what you are saying. Not only that, you are much more likely to have your work shared if you add in some pictures. According to research by Adobe / Software Advice images are the most important factor in optimal social media content. Over 80% of survey respondents said visuals were either "Very Important" or "Important" for their marketing optimisation on social.

I tend to stress about the choice of picture as much as the headline and will often spend as much time foraging for a spectacular image as I did writing the article in the first place.

I try to adhere to certain rules when I am hunting down an image. First and foremost, you need to try and seek out images that are rights-free. There are plenty of copyright free sites available for images – you don't need me to list them, especially as there are new ones being created all the time. Just give it a quick Google and there will be plenty of them listed for you to take a look at.

Before you start to track down your image, read through your piece again and try to get a mental image of the picture you are looking for. Chances are that you will not end up with what you originally had in mind but it's a strong starting point. And when you have that image in mind, use it to filter similar images. You might find (as I often do) it will be one of the associated images that will probably be your final selection.

The biggest mistake that people make is selecting a terminally dull photo. I see lazy choices every day when it comes to use of images: even if you have an intriguing title for your piece you don't give it a fighting chance unless you select an equally interesting visual to go with it. Many people clearly don't believe it's important and will randomly use clip-art or a generic picture of smiling business people or (even worse) some kind of pie chart or graph. All completely useless choices.

Other ones that definitely don't work? Pictures that are too detailed. Remember a lot of people use their smartphone to access LinkedIn, so given the relatively small size of that screen you need to ensure that the image you choose is simple and clear. Always try and look at your chosen image on your phone first to see if it 'pops' out of the screen.

Which also brings me to a few very basic points (so basic they shouldn't really need mentioning but it would be remiss of me if I didn't). Make sure the image you have selected has a decent resolution. Anything less than about 2MB is probably going to look grainy and pixelated. And don't ever use anything with a watermark. Obviously if you are using those images it means they are not rights-free and also it just looks amateurish.

All too often I see images that have been selected which have absolutely nothing to do with the subject matter. Now that's okay if you are desperately trying to be cryptic, but in my experience it actually serves to confuse rather than illuminate. Remember, you have a mere fraction of a second to capture a readers attention so don't make it too difficult for them to try and match the content to the image.

If the tonality of the piece is strong, then again try and reflect that in the image. For the most part, as I have mentioned previously, my articles tend to be amusing (or at least I like to think so). Therefore, I often try to pick a photo that is a little quirky, offbeat or (to me at least) just plain funny.

So that's the main image taken care of. Now what about within the article itself?

Well this is a personal choice but I really like to punctuate my item with a variety of pictures to embellish what I am saying. Again, the same rules apply - try and make them dynamic, otherwise there is just no point. In any one piece that I write, there will be as many as ten images to help tell the story. It's often as a summary to a paragraph where I have made a specific statement and I use the visual to add depth and colour to that commentary. It can be time consuming but I believe that it's worth the extra effort if the comments from my readers and followers are anything to go by. On occasion they talk about the visuals I have chosen rather than the piece itself.

I can't show any examples of my favourite images in this book (I opted for the basic text version instead of the rather more expensively produced colour / bleed version) but you can always take a look at my LinkedIn profile for some strong examples of what I mean. Look up some of my favourites such as the picture of Dolly Parton for the article '9 to 5 is NO way to make a Living' or the man taking a selfie with a shark for 'Me, My Selfie & Die'.

Publish according to Time Zone

When I first starting publishing on LinkedIn, I was based in Singapore in a role which covered Asia Pacific. So naturally, I thought that the majority of my audience would come from APAC. How wrong I was.

After just a couple of weeks writing, I ventured into the analytics section of LinkedIn Publishing and started to interrogate some of the statistics provided. I was astounded to discover that despite my initial assumption that my audience would be from markets like Singapore, China, India and Australia it was predominantly from the United States. Generally speaking it was New York followed closely by Los Angeles and San Francisco. On average I discovered that the U.S represented around 40% of my audience.

Interestingly though, I had been posting most of my initial articles to coincide with the working day in Asia. Given that my work was gaining more traction in the States, I decided to recalibrate my publishing schedule to see if it had any effect. Through a period of basic trial and error where I tested the initial posting at different times of day, it became very clear that if I published my items at the start of the working day in the U.S then my viewing numbers were significantly higher. When I posted at around 9am EST it yielded the best response. Of course, it is heavily dependent on the subject matter as well but there was a discernable increase in traffic by adopting this simple technique.

So am I suggesting that you do exactly the same and start chasing the American audience? Well that's really up to you. It definitely makes sense if you are based in the USA but you might prefer to build up a core readership in your own country. If that's the case then ensure that you are posting on your own time zone. Sometimes though, your decision on when to post can be driven by your subject matter. For instance, I wrote a piece about a new platform for Sky TV in the UK so obviously I geared that to coincide with the start of the British working day. Similarly, for an article I wrote about India (which is actually featured in the very next section) I made sure that it was published at the beginning of the day in Mumbai.

Best Day of the Week?

Selecting the best day of the week to publish is very much linked to the time of day and time zone you want to get most noticed. Again, you can maybe benefit from the hit-and-miss approach that I have adopted over the past year since LinkedIn launched their platform.

I have experimented with posts across the week to see if there was any difference in response. Now, I don't have any real science to back up my claims but I do have plenty of reader comments to back up my opinion. Generally speaking if your subject matter is quite serious then it tends to work better at the outset of the week. When the weekend is over and the working week is grinding inexorably back into action, I would say that the mindset of the business community is more receptive to a hard-hitting article. For example the article below was written as a follow-up to my piece on the Chinese economy. It was published on a Monday geared towards the start of the working day in India and the LinkedIn analytics demonstrate that the tactic worked. The highest audience came from India...

Will India benefit the most from the faltering Chinese economy?

My recent article *'Forget Greece, the real financial crisis is happening in China'* certainly struck a chord with LinkedIn readers - it was viewed almost 20,000 times. Since that piece, the financial stability of the Chinese economy has (at best) been somewhat volatile, which prompted a question. Who might benefit? And the simple answer appears to be India...

The woes in the Chinese stock exchange have been well documented so I won't bore you by repeating them yet again. But other economic indicators reported out of Beijing this week add more doom and gloom to an already bleak outlook. Consumer price inflation slowed in China much more than anticipated in September which clearly reflects weak domestic demand. In the same month, it was reported that imports had fallen by around 20%. And, in my humble opinion, the most interesting indicator of China's slowdown? Luxury brand Louis Vuitton admitted this week that they were feeling the pinch and blamed their sluggish sales on China. Their CFO, Jean-Jacques Guiony, made it very clear to investors:

"This is obviously connected with what happened in China in July and August in the stock market. We know perfectly well that when asset depreciation of such a magnitude takes place, this has an impact on our business, and China was no exception. The

drop in the stock market has taken its toll."

So as China continues to falter, does this provide the opportunity that India have been seeking to reignite their own stop / start economy? Well, the media certainly seems to think it's time for India to step up and take their chance. Various reports in the Wall Street Journal, CNN etc. have suggested that because of the recent economic turmoil in China they claim that India can overtake them as the <u>driver</u> of the world economy.

Consumer spending in India has remained remarkably resilient which gives them a distinct advantage as demand has decelerated in most other markets. India has also been increasingly successful in luring companies to manufacture their products in India and the government is pinning their hopes on a belated industrial revolution capitalising on their vast 1.2 billion population. The Wall Street Journal picked up on this point and stated that:

"For years, growth in India has been fuelled more by domestic demand not, as in China, by manufacturing goods for sale abroad. India hasn't been rattled as badly as Brazil, Russia or South Africa. Its international reserves are ample and it isn't highly dependent on foreign capital to fund imports"

In a deft stroke of timing, Indian Prime Minister Narendra Modi, launched the highly enterprising 'Make in India' initiative just over a year ago supported with a high profile marketing campaign. It is already yielding positive results, the latest of which was announced just this week with (somewhat ironically) Chinese smartphone manufacturer Gionee committing to making their first handset in India. It is predicted that by 2020, electronics and hardware demand will be worth $400 billion in the country with smartphones accounting for almost 40% of that demand.

Modi has also been courting the US market specifically and it appears to be paying off. US Under Secretary of Commerce, Stefan Selig, said in a visit to India last month that because the US produces *"the best manufacturing exports"* India will have *"no better partner"* in its bid to make the country *"an elite manufacturing hub on the global stage."* Selig went on to say that the most important goal in India-US collaboration is to aim for a fivefold increase in the annual bilateral trade from the current $100 billion to $500 billion. A big ask and some eye-watering numbers although he didn't mention a time frame...

But not everyone is so enamoured by the claims that India are to emerge from the China crisis as front runners in world trade. An article in the Financial Times pours scorn on the various reports and dismisses the optimism as *schadenfreude...*

One of main reasons cited by the FT is that India is benefiting in the short term due to the global collapse of commodity prices, particularly oil which they need to import in vast quantities. The article also goes on to criticise the transport infrastructure in India which is still relatively poor when compared to China and could easily prevent significant investment from wary industrial groups. Their conclusion?

"India, in short, does indeed enjoy opportunities arising from China's problems and the external economic environment, but will not be able to take advantage of them

unless it quickly tackles its own domestic challenges"

So what do you think? Is this the time for the global economic spotlight to shine on India or are they simply not ready for it yet?

The start of the week was an appropriate time to publish about this weightier subject matter and achieved it's objective of attracting an audience from key Indian cities.

However, after the mid-week hump has been breached then people seem to be more open to something a little more, shall we say, frivolous. I wrote this next example late on a Thursday evening after a particularly gruelling day of back-to-back conference calls. I was going to wait until the following week to publish it but decided on a whim that it might make some light reading on a Friday morning. I'm glad I didn't wait because it did decent numbers...

5 reasons why I HATE conference calls

Conference calls are the bane of my life (and if you are reading this, I'm guessing maybe yours too?). They have become so clichéd that spoof versions are being produced by resourceful comedians - check out the genius *A Conference Call in Real Life* which has over 10 million hits on YouTube.

So why do I detest them so much? Here is my top 5 list of loathes...

1. *The 'Mute' Point* - which is not a moot point (see what I did there?) in my humble opinion... it doesn't seem to matter how many times people have been on a conference call, or how many times they are reminded at the start of them, there is always at least one person who ignores the etiquette of muting their phone whilst other people are speaking.

Then just to compound the problem, they are also the ones who decide it's the perfect opportunity to chow down on some corn chips. And there is nothing we like better than listening intently to someone shovel down their Dorito's and dips right? RIGHT??

2. *The 'Baskervilles' Syndrome* - linked to the above, we have all witnessed the errant pooch who never so much as whimpers when someone is breaking into your home but at the merest sign of you lifting a handset to your ear turns into the *Hound of the Baskervilles*. Lumped into the same category go all children who haven't uttered a syllable all day but suddenly decide that the commencement of your Webex is the perfect time to start their drum practice...

3. *The Twilight Zone* - particularly prevalent if you work in Asia and have to attend Global concalls. To accommodate all the regions, the

only time that works for the guys in APAC is at night. Just what you need after a long hard day at the coal face. At least the team in the US are freshly rested and in EMEA it's right in the middle of their working day. Throw in a dash of jetlag after a long trip and I am embarrassed to admit that I once fell asleep during one such call. Now, that wouldn't have been quite so bad if I had remembered rule number 1 and muted my phone (I never said I wasn't guilty did I?). Waking up at the desk in my hotel room with my phone still in my hand was pretty bad. Much worse though was the gleeful email from one of my colleagues telling me that they had all heard the dull thud of my head hitting the table followed a brief groan and an hour or so of (not so) gentle snoring.

4. *The Feedback Phenomenon* - now, as a hard rock aficionado I am rather partial to listening to the likes of Eddie Van Halen

making his guitar wail by pointing his pickups in the direction of a stack of smoking Marshalls. On a conference call though? Not so much. And as good as your latest Panasonic DECT office phone may be, put it too close to the concall speaker it still doesn't quite have the same spine-tingling feedback feel as EvH belting out Eruption.

5. *The Time Thief* - I have a (admittedly, less than robust) theory that conference calls create some kind of wormhole in the space time continuum which basically means that no matter how long a call is scheduled for, it will inevitably take at least twice as long. Your Outlook says it will last for 30 minutes? Never. In concall parlance that really means at least an hour. Why? Because inevitably there will be at least one person who joins late. Then they feel compelled to apologise and proceed (unprompted) to tell everyone why. Which eats up more time. And if they

joined less than 5 minutes late the speaker will most likely offer to begin again. And then after a few minutes someone else will join late. Wash. Rinse. Repeat. Factor in all the other delays (people talking over each other, participants dropping out of the call, dialling back in, apologising and explaining that they are half way up a palm tree to get a signal etc.etc.) then it's no wonder that they never run to the allotted time.

So there you have it, my top 5 pet peeves with concalls. Have you got any more to add to the collection?

Now in truth I've read a few articles that suggest an alternative to my theory. For example, there is a counter argument that the best days to post on LinkedIn are midweek from Tuesday to Thursday. According to their findings Monday is not a good day to post content for maximising views, because most professionals are getting back into the daily grind (so in fact the complete opposite to what I have observed!).

They may have a point but it's difficult to prove either way. I suspect that LinkedIn are far more aware of the reality but are unlikely to tell their publishing community because then we would all publish on the same day at the same time wouldn't we?

I still play around with the variables to see if I can learn more about the various permutations of time to publish. It may also be true that in your chosen field, the rhythm of the week is different, so my advice to you would be to challenge yourself to keep experimenting and find out what works best for your writing.

The use of the 'Listicle'

Why are we all suckers for a list? Whether it be a Top 10 Tips or a more comprehensive A to Z we love our information spliced and diced for us into handy bite sized chunks. Social media has amplified the importance of the listicle (as it now often referred to) with Buzzfeed-style snackable content being the short order of the day.

It would be churlish then not to tell you the 9 reasons why people love to assimilate their information in an ordered fashion and naturally the best way to do that is, of course, via a listicle:

o We know what we are getting – psychologists call this 'schemata' which are basically mental shortcuts which allow us to understand and process information more easily
o Fear of missing out – a listicle is an easy-to-spot social currency because it suggests that

valuable content is super accessible and shareable which encourages you to click

o Less taxing on the brain – a densely worded article is daunting for many individuals, so anything that makes reading less of a chore works for us

o Easier to 'scan' – the readers of lists again will often take a short cut and quickly scan through the list of vital pieces of information and then read the entire piece if it really interests them. A longer narrative is much more difficult to skim read

o We know how much is left – we like to know roughly how long it is before we finish an article and people automatically estimate how long it will take to read the piece once they have started

o We like to guess the outcomes – research studies conclude that we like to guess the contents of a list because the brain rewards us with a kick of dopamine

- We love being right – and that surge of dopamine is enhanced further if we correctly manage to ascertain any of the answers
- A list is definitive – by packaging information into a list it gives us a sense that everything is settled and complete. We don't like uncertainty as that means a lack of control

It's a simple trick, used on a regular basis by many writers on LinkedIn. But a word of caution, don't use this method on every single occasion as it can become tiresome when over-deployed. Personally speaking, I have been trying to limit the number of lists I write to roughly one in every five items just so that I don't get too dependent upon them. Trust me, it is hard to avoid them because they do tend to work rather well.

Here is an example listicle that I wrote in the first week of 2016, which details five New Year resolutions that you should make (and try not to break):

5 New Year 'Work' Resolutions you should make… but will almost inevitably break?

Did you know that 92% of all New Year resolutions fail? Why do we start each year with a mandate to be better, remain resolute for a few weeks in January, falter in February and fully forget them by March? Maybe it's because they are personal goals which are simply unrealistic and too difficult to achieve (quit smoking after 20 years, lose half your body weight etc.). So what about 'work resolutions' instead? Are they more attainable than personal goals or are they just as likely to be scrapped by the Spring?

So I've put together a listicle of 5 work related resolutions which I reckon (with a little effort) we can all respond to:

1. Lock & Load - get serious and set yourself an achievable target for the next 12 months then formulate a proper plan on how you intend to succeed. Make it something that can enhance your career. Want that promotion? Well figure out what it takes to get it. Is it improved sales, a better relationship with your colleagues, being more sociable ? Set yourself some personal KPI's, align them to your work ones and make them specific (e.g. if it's a sales increase put a number or percentage against it). It's all about the preparation. And you know what a certain Mr Benjamin Franklin said about that...

As for me? Well I have set myself the task of writing a book. Yeah I know, I know, I know... the people who say that are a dime a dozen. But I am definitely going for it. It is my first (and possibly last) but as the saying goes 'everyone has a book in them'.

Maybe not a very good one, but a book nonetheless. Or at least a pamphlet. Anyway now is the time for me to take mine from my head and put it on the page. I've already completed the outline, contacted a publisher and written the first chapter (and the Christmas turkey is barely cold). What's the book about? Check back in a year to find out. But one thing is for sure, I <u>will</u> have it published.

So, for what its worth, that's my 2016 goal - the real question is, what is yours and what are you going to do to make it a reality?

2. Make more time for 'me' - well not 'me' exactly but you. Am I making this overly complicated?

But be warned if you try and <u>find</u> the time you will fail by February. You need to <u>make</u> the time to succeed.

I think it's fair to say that U.S President Barack Obama is a pretty busy chap. I'd warrant that he is even busier than you and I. Put together. Yet he has carved out three moments in his daily schedule that are undeniably about 'him'. His morning workout, dinner with his family and some downtime after they have gone to sleep. Each time segment serves a specific purpose for Obama:

- exercise keeps his body (and mind) in the peak of health

- the family dinner is his most sacred time and provides him with some genuine perspective on his life and work

- the 'after hours' slot helps him catch up, read a book, listen to music and prepare for the next day

Simply put, you don't have to run a marathon or scale a tall building in a single bound to succeed in this space. Just do what you love whether it be meditation, colouring books, playing guitar or whatever. It will reap its own rewards in terms of that much vaunted work/life balance.

Personally, I am determined to travel less this year and spend a little more time with family and friends. Last year I was away about 30 weeks. This year, I'm aiming for less than 20. Although given that I am away for the next two, maybe not the most auspicious of starts. Ah well, it's a marathon not a sprint...

3. Dare to delegate - empowerment is a powerful tool. As former Apple CEO Steve Jobs famously said:

"it doesn't make sense to hire smart people and tell them what to do; we hire smart people so they can tell us what to do."

I was lucky enough to go on a senior management course to Babson a few years ago and was 'schooled' by some incredibly influential professors from Harvard University. One of the (many) things they taught us was that, as business leaders, we consistently fall into the trap of assuming we can do it all. The simple and undeniable truth is that we can't. It's a common cliche but there are only so many hours in the day and you cannot possibly achieve everything you want. Not only that but if you steadfastly stick to the opinion that only you can do what is necessary to get the job done then it will inevitably breed resentment with your colleagues.

And the best piece of advice given by the lecturers? Teach yourself to trade off the things that others can do better than you. It's a matter of trust and respect (to your colleagues and to yourself). And frankly, to echo the point of Mr Jobs, if you can't / won't / don't trust or respect them, then why did you hire them in the first place?

4. Old dog, new tricks - trying to learn something new will not only add to your skills it will bring a different dimension to your life. In addition, it will potentially introduce you to a whole World of new and fascinating people who in turn may become colleagues, customers or even friends.

Last year, I challenged myself to step up my writing and publish at least once a week on various platforms including LinkedIn (as pushed by my pal Andrew Goldman). And the result? I was named as a *LinkedIn Top Voice for 2015* in addition to *Agency Publisher of the Year* for EMEA. Consequently, I now have a slew of new followers (over 4000) and some really promising discussions with a few of those people to take matters to the next level - as I mentioned earlier in this piece, to get a book published. See how quickly these things can escalate?

On top of that, as I work a lot in France, I want to brush up my, err, language skills. In all honesty, I've never been much good at speaking French. Enthusiastic at best, I can manage to give a taxi driver directions but beyond that I am pretty clueless. So, I have set myself a challenge to at least be able to have a conversation with my work colleagues. Mon dieu et zut alors.

So what new skill can an 'old dog' like you learn and how could it change your business life for the better?

5. Learn to let go - take a long, cold hard look at yourself when you are conducting business. Is there a technique, a product or a business relationship that just isn't working for you? Be honest, if that's the case then (in the inimitable words of the modern day Disney classic) *"Let it Go"*. Chances are that it's likely to be a long term thing and you are simply bound by habit. But what is the point in investing valuable time, energy and resource into trying to make the unworkable workable. It's time to wise up and move on.

My biggest vice? Powerpoint. I use it as a panacea for all ills. But it isn't, as I highlighted in a previous article entitled *Does Powerpoint Make You*

Stupid? Our over reliance on the PPT has become insane to the extent that we punctuate our business lives with needless bullet points. My plan for 2016 is to find viable alternatives - and I don't mean Prezi or Keynote. Maybe it's props, or miming or improv (ok so possibly I'm getting a bit carried away now) but I am going to try and find some new interface to communicate with clients.

So there you have it, 5 New Year work resolutions. Will I succeed in achieving all of these? And will you with yours? Well I, for one, am seriously going to try. But knowing me (and I do, reasonably well) then learning French will almost inevitably be my proverbial 'achilles heel' and I confidently predict that "je vais echouer par Avril". See what I mean? Useless.

And if you read that through you will see that I kept at least one of my New Year resolutions – and this is the very book that I made a commitment to write. As for speaking French though... erm...

Why use Tagging?

I made a plethora of errors when I initially started publishing on LinkedIn and I have already pointed out quite a few. This is yet another one to add to the (already) long laundry list of faux pas.

Frankly, I didn't even realise that you could tag your articles when I first started writing. My excuse is that I was unfamiliar with the format. That isn't much of an excuse though is it? Ignorance is not a 'get out of jail free' card.

Tagging is invaluable for two reasons: firstly, because it helps you find the right audience for your piece, and secondly because it gives the article a far better chance of being picked up by the editors (via the complex series of algorithms) and therefore featured in their various channels on LinkedIn Pulse. That alone can make a huge difference to the volume of views you will achieve as I have mentioned previously. Now that I am a more established writer, the chances of my work being selected have increased significantly but I am never blasé about it. I always think carefully about where I think my work will fit into the many categories that are available. Whenever you write, try to think about how it can be categorised. To be blunt, if your work is so niche that it cannot be tagged in some way then it will simply wither on the vine. Harsh, but true.

To give you a helping hand, I have identified the categories with the strongest followings on LinkedIn:

- *Leadership & Management – 12.9 million*
- *Big Ideas & Innovation – 11.1 million*
- *Technology – 9.5 million*
- *Entrepreneurship – 7.7 million*
- *Social Media – 7.2 million*
- *Economy – 7.0 million*
- *Professional Women – 6.8 million*
- *Marketing & Advertising – 6.4 million*
- *Green Business – 3.6 million*
- *Banking & Finance – 3.6 million*

- *Best Advice – 3.3 million*
- *Education – 3.0 million*
- *Customer Experience – 2.7 million*
- *Healthcare – 2.6 million*
- *Recruiting & Hiring – 2.6 million*
- *Big Data – 2.3 million*
- *Your Career – 2.2 million*

If you want to write about something that's a little more offbeat you are likely to get a smaller but fiercer audience - but if you want it to reach a broader audience then try and make your article fit into one of these top channels.

I used this method to great effect in an article I published in February 2016 on the growing scourge of silly mathematical puzzles on Facebook and (increasingly to my annoyance) on LinkedIn. Anyway, the point I want to make here is that with judicious choice of appropriate tagging I managed to secure some reasonably high viewing numbers. I opted for three tags that were closely associated with Big Ideas

& Innovation plus (unsurprisingly) Social Media. As a consequence, the editors quickly picked up the article and it was featured in both sections:

Why is this kids puzzle driving the internet bananas? (and why YOU can't solve it)

(12,446 Views, 630 Likes, 227 Comments)

This simple brain teaser has taken Facebook by storm. Now it's infiltrated LinkedIn as well. But why? It's so easy to solve. Or is it?

At first glance it's a pretty obvious algebraic equation. Now bear with me whilst we go through the logic. The first line demonstrates that three apples added together is 30. So surely 1 apple is equal to 10. Any arguments? Nope? OK so lets move on.

Then we see that 1 apple (10) added to 2 bunches of bananas equals 18. Basic maths indicates that each bunch of bananas is equal to 4. 10+4+4=18

So far, so good?

Then the next line says that a bunch of bananas (as we have established, a value of 4) minus 2 half coconuts equals 2
therefore suggesting that the coconuts are the equivalent to 2.

Right then, so on the last line, it requests the answer to the sum of one half a coconut (1) plus one apple (10) and a bunch of bananas (4). 1+10+4=15. Problem solved, vague sense of smugness, share to see if your friends are as 'smart' as you are and move on right? Wrong.

It seems that we are not maybe as observant as we'd like to think and that we have been duped by our own complacency. If you take a closer look at the bananas, you will see that the bunches are not equal. The bunches in the second and third lines have 4 bananas but in the last line there are only 3 bananas. So if that's the case, then the value of each banana should be 1 and hence the value of the last bunch of bananas should be 3 which means that the final answer should actually be 14.

So there we have it, problem solved. Not so fast Sherlock. Now you need to inspect those nuts more closely... If you peek more intently you might notice that the 2 halves of coconut are not identical. The left half is different to the right half. And the half that is featured in the final equation is only the left half. The question is then, are the values of each half coconut different because they are not identical?

2.2 million people have left their answers and shared the picture which has become a viral sensation with increasingly wild (and often stupid) solutions being proffered. So what do the experts say? Well Dr Kevin Bowman, Mathematics expert at the University of Central Lancashire is quoted as saying:

"You can interpret it in many ways; one way is no more correct than another. There's no ambiguity in the first equation; 3 apples is 30, so one apple is worth 10. But because all the bananas aren't the same, you could say that they all represent different amounts. You might even say that the two coconut pieces in the third equation are different sizes, and therefore add up to three quarters or even seven eighths when put together. In that sense, there are an infinite amount of possible answers"

So I've had a really good think about it and figured something out. I don't know the answer and frankly I don't care. My solution? Don't waste your time on stupid s*** like this. Takes all the fun out of a simple fruit salad.

Hyperlink - a lot

Although I knew the hyperlink option was available in the toolbar on LinkedIn Publishing, I never really saw the need for it when I began writing articles. Again it was Andy Goldman who mentioned that I needed to utilise the function more often as it would have a beneficial effect on my viewing figures.

Once again, time has proven him to be correct. Come on Andy, no one likes a smart ass.

On a slightly more serious note, I have found that the extensive usage of hyperlinks pays off in a number of ways. Firstly, if you are referencing an article or source using a link it adds credibility to what you are saying. The reader can easily authenticate any of your facts, figures, or quotes for themselves at the click of a button.

In addition, it can significantly help drive traffic to your piece via Google search. According to research from the likes of MozCast, using links in any form of long or short form content can drive traffic by an average of around 6% and even as high as 10%. I have checked the number on my posts and the reality is that I get around 2% of my views via Google search but that's still a healthy number overall and certainly worth maintaining and even cultivating.

And finally, you can use hyperlinks to add a dash of creativity to your posts. For instance, when Apple Music declared their plans to offer an all-you-can-eat music service to rival the likes of Spotify, I decided to write something about it. As I was putting it together a thought occurred to me. I wondered if I could make all of my points built around songs and then hyperlink them to videos of those same tracks on YouTube? And that's precisely what I did... I present to you (what I believe to be) the first (and probably last) ever LinkedIn post to be almost exclusively strung together with music tracks. How many can you spot?

Spotify vs Apple - The Final Countdown?

"The perfect music should always be just a touch away" said Spotify CEO Daniel Ek at a news conference last week. So if that's the case, as the world's largest music-streaming service, why are they still losing 'Money, Money, Money' and having to adapt their offering to include video?

Since their launch 4 years ago, Spotify has been a 'Revelation' in the 'Music' industry by offering an 'all-you-can-eat' smorgasbord of music for a one-off monthly fee or as an ad-based free alternative. To date, they have amassed a user base of around 60 million with around 45 million adopting the free version and the remaining 15 million signed up to the Premium paid version. All of which has changed the dynamic of music listening 'Forever' - as digital downloads continue to decline, streaming has soared by 54% in the past year alone.

With over US $1 billion in revenue and a company valuation of US $ 8 billion you would guess that their business was pretty lucrative right? Wrong. The reality is that Spotify is not profitable. And their losses are actually increasing. I wonder if they will ever get 'Back in Black' ?

'Why' are they losing money then? Well it's mainly due to the onerous costs of the content / royalties that they have to pay to the publishers (estimated to be in the region of 70% of it's revenue). And the 'Problem' is, that no matter how huge their user base grows that ratio is unlikely to change dramatically. 'You Can't Always Get What You Want' right?

It has also spawned a whole host of platforms who were 'Born This Way' such as Deezer, (Bohemian) Rhapsody, Pandora, Rdio and Tidal to name but a few. However, the one they need really worry about.? Apple. Last year they paid $ US 3 billion for Beats, the premium headphone and streaming business. So far there has only been the 'Sound of Silence' about their plans for Beats. The industry has been 'Looking for Clues' but so far we have little idea as to what it will look (or should that be sound) like.

What we do know is that it is likely to be a 'Monster.' Apple already have details of over 800 million credit cards on file from their existing iTunes customer base. That 'Alone' gives them the capability to entirely reshape the streaming music landscape again if they can come up with an effective new 'Model.' One possible theory is that Apple could use music as a loss leader to 'Drive' sales of their hardware. 'Imagine' that - all of your music included with the purchase of an iPhone or iPad? It's like 'Money for Nothing.' And your music (and chips) for free?

In 'Anticipation' of any potential move by Apple, Spotify have evidently decided to diversify by adding video and podcasts to their armoury of streamed services with a new offering called Spotify Now. To all intents and purposes, Spotify wants to become the entertainment destination for '24 Hour Party People' – essentially a central conduit for all 'That's Entertainment' based content which consumers want on their mobile device. And they have decided to 'Hook Up' with some major video content suppliers (eg. BBC, NBC, ESPN, Comedy Central etc.) to deliver the video element of their offering. 'God Only Knows' if that group of content providers can 'Help!' deliver the quality content that their consumers are seeking.

But by entering the domain of video, they are 'Opening' themselves up to a whole new set of competitors. Not least, the colossal Google and their video platform YouTube. It will be difficult to 'Beat It.' Not only that but it seems everyone is jumping on the video bandwagon of late, so they will also have to contend with other tech behemoths like Facebook and Snapchat (via Discover) plus more established platforms like Hulu and Roku.

They also announced a raft of consumer focused partnership deals to enhance their business. For example they have penned a deal with Nike to link their running app with Spotify playlists (the music choices can automatically adapt to your running speed). In addition, they have signed up with Starbucks who are going to 'Stop' selling CD's in store and instead will offer their 10 million Starbucks loyalty program members a 'Reward' to redeem against free drinks for simply listening to specially curated music playlists. 'At the End of the Line' we need to revisit the original premise of this piece. Spotify is ostensibly a music service - as Daniel Ek himself stated this week:

> *"we are a technology company by design, but we are really a music company at heart"*

But if that's the case then they have clearly recognised that there are limitations to this in 'The Future' by being single-mindedly focused on being a music platform. Diversify or die. But on the 'The Other Side' whilst they want to provide 'Common People' with everything, we all have our own unique requirements. Anything extraneous to that becomes unnecessary background noise which could cause a 'State of Confusion' with potential new recruits and equally may alienate existing users who just want it for the their tunes. As Dan Cryan, analyst at researcher IHS, puts it:

On one hand, you're going mass-market by giving consumers more options. But if you make the core product harder to use, then you actually begin to remove the reason why a lot of your users are there in the first place"

Hmm, could be a case of 'Video Killed the Radio Star?'

So here's the thing, it didn't do brilliantly in terms of viewing. It didn't even break through 500, wasn't picked up by the editors and only had a paltry 8 comments. It also took ages to construct it (more than twice as long as usual as I was thinking about how I could incorporate tunes for the entire time) plus it also took forever to add in all of those pesky links.

But sometimes, just sometimes, it's not exclusively about the numbers. On this occasion I wrote it because I thought it was a quirky idea and it had never been done before (not that I could find anyway). Remember to always try to write for yourself. It was also really good fun. I was laughing out loud as I was writing it and that is a reward in itself. And finally, and most gratifying, the comments I received were some of my favourites as they carried on with the same song title theme.

Sharing on other Social Platforms (Twitter, Facebook etc.)

If you have published previously on the LinkedIn platform, you will have already noticed that as soon as you hit the 'Publish' button you are provided with two additional options to share your piece on either Facebook or Twitter. I always do both. And why not? If you really want to maximise the audience you are reaching then it's vital you utilise as many channels as possible.

I have elicited a decent response from both of these avenues. Again the stats that are kindly provided by LinkedIn show the top traffic sources and Facebook, for example, delivers on average anything between 1%-5% of the total views. The following example did particularly well via Facebook but I guess that's not so surprising given that the subject of the piece was Facebook...

Who asks the World's toughest interview question? (and how would YOU answer it?)

The toughest question asked at an interview is posed by Facebook according to a recent *Business Insider* article. Why? Because Mark Zuckerberg will...

"only hire someone to work directly for me if I would work for that person"

Miranda Kalinowski (Facebook's Global Head of Recruiting) and Lori Goler (Vice President of People Operations) concocted the killer question for prospective candidates to help them secure talent who are a 'perfect fit' for their organisation. Asking interviewees mundane questions about their previous work experience (yawn), getting them to (often falsely) wax lyrical about their 'best qualities' and probing them on (that old chestnut) their 'biggest failings' do not exist in the Facebook recruiting guide. I think it's fair to say their method is a tad more unconventional...

They initially soften up candidates with a few punchy inquiries such as:

"how do you manage work if you lose track of the time?"

Well I'm always losing track of time but I still manage to do my work. Am I missing the point here?

Anyway, then they quiz candidates across a range of 5 key topics including:

1. Comfort zones: Basically, forget them. Goler got her job at Facebook by

cold-calling Sheryl Sandberg (who, in case you didn't know, is Facebook's COO). Goler's opening gambit? *"I want to help Facebook achieve its mission. Whatever that means for Facebook is what I'm happy to do."* Ballsy right? Or desperate? Depends on your perspective I suppose. Just one query - how did she get Sandberg's number to cold call her?

2. Codification: you don't have to be a code master but a passing knowledge of Javascript wouldn't do you any harm it seems (that's me out then)

3. Being Bolder: in Facebook parlance they are seeking someone who utilises the tools of their trade in smart and previously unimaginable ways ('smart' I can't do but I could have a decent shot at 'unimaginable')

4. **Self Management: don't expect to be told what to do at Facebook. Minimal supervision and flexible hours are the order of the day. As long as you yield results of course (take a look at my previous article *'Working 9to5 is No Way to Make a Living'* for more on that very topic)**

5. **Daring to be Different: thinking outside of the proverbial box naturally but also 'diversity' is currently a hot topic in the tech world**

And finally (thanks for being so patient, dear reader, but if I had told you earlier then wouldn't have read this far would you?) we get to that elusive million dollar question. Well not actually a million bucks per se, but an average salary of around $170,000 per annum at Facebook according to various sources. So without further ado, the World's toughest interview question is (silent drum roll):

"On your very best day at work... the day you come home and think you have the best job in the world... what did you do that day?"

There you go then, that's the big one. So are you over or under whelmed? It matters not a jot, that's the question and that's all there is to it.

As for the correct answer? Well come on, Facebook are not going to divulge that are they? Although they do kindly offer a clue. If your response coincides with Facebook's mission *'to give people the power to share and make the world more open and connected'* (whatever that means) then you have a more than decent chance of progressing to the next round.

So, I have given this an awful lot of thought (roughly about a minute) and I reckon that I have come up with a most awesome reply. Now I will concede that time to think (even for just a minute) is a luxury that potential employees don't receive in the white heat intensity of an interview with Facebook. Still, if they are giving away their HR secrets then I'm going to capitalise on the opportunity. And so here it is, my absolutely definitive and (I personally believe) almost perfect answer to their most vexing interview question:

"I totally screwed up... but I didn't get found out"

Totally nailed it. Now Lori, what is Sheryl Sandberg's phone number?

Hang on though. Not convinced by my answer? To be honest, me neither. So how would you answer it?

You won't be shocked to hear that I really focused on Facebook shares for this item and encouraged others to share on the same platform. As you can see from the high number of views, that strategy worked rather well.

However, your sharing shouldn't stop there. There are a multitude of other options to consider beyond the humble tweet or Facebook share. Wherever you believe you can build an audience, take the time to cultivate one. The social landscape is constantly evolving so it's pretty much impossible to provide a definitive list of opportunities at any point in time (as soon as you had finished, the list would most likely be out of date). So I'm not going to even attempt to provide an exhaustive list but a few that you should have on your radar include the likes of Google+, Instagram, Pinterest, Tumblr, Flickr and so on.

And if you want to go one stage further, you can also consider various online apps / tools which help manage your various social networking accounts from one centralised dashboard.

Another neat tactic I have employed from time to time is harnessing the power of your friends, colleagues and acquaintances networks by including them in the pieces that you write about. Most of us have been lucky enough to have worked with, become mates with or at least been introduced to some very influential people across a variety of industries. They themselves have very powerful communities all of their own which could be an extremely strong source of readers for you. So ask yourself the question, who in your personal list of connections could you ask to provide a killer quote for your next article? Of course it has to be someone who is an expert on the topic you are writing about and equally has the gravitas to make an audience take note.

I have used a variety of connections depending on the type of article I am writing. One such example is Chris van Someren, who is a global talent management expert and CEO of Ascentador. I have asked Chris for his opinion on a few occasions, specifically when I am making a point about (amongst other things) Human Resources. For example, for an article I feature later in the book about why I believe LinkedIn is making resumes obsolete Chris offered some exceptional insights into the matter from the perspective of someone who knows that side of the business inside out. Not only that but because he has been quoted he has been more than willing to share the item with his connections thereby granting me privileged access to his extended network and all with the added benefit of his valuable endorsement.

Inspired by the response to those articles, Chris now publishes regularly on LinkedIn:

"Publishing on LinkedIn has helped to uplift and enlarge our ongoing conversation with our network. Not only does LinkedIn help to ensure that the broadest possible audience is exposed to our

content, but it consistently fosters and enables a response, enhances the depth of our existing relationships, and invites even 'strangers' to know us better"

So make the best of your existing contacts to help you push out your content and maybe even encourage them to do the same with you and assist them in gaining a wider audience.

Join relevant Groups

Or even some irrelevant ones if you wish but do join some groups. By becoming part of these groups you can expand your reader base significantly and have a regular dialogue with them. According to LinkedIn's own figures writers can boost their viewing numbers fivefold by ensuring that they are part of some relevant groups.

I began exclusively with groups that were related to the industry in which I work. I joined all the media, advertising and communications variants that I could find. They have proved to provide a rich vein of readers especially for pieces such as this:

'Creative' Business Leader? You have no idea

(4,744 Views, 744 Likes, 40 Comments)

Common convention tells us that the best business leaders are creative, innovative and

dynamic thinkers. Right? Wrong. According to a study featured in the Harvard Business Review their capacity to ideate is no better than the rest of us mere mortals. Let them lead a brainstorm session and apparently their performance will be worse than if they collaborated equally.

The research conducted by the University of California Berkeley proves that leaders are less productive when asked to lead others whilst ideating and are actually more likely to generate conflict within a group than their compatriots.

Berkeley boffins Angus Hildreth and Cameron Anderson produced four studies which specifically tested how high-powered individuals perform in a creative thinking task.

The main task was simple. Work in a team of 3 to create a fictional new organisation and then create a strategy on how to run it (sounds a lot like 'The Apprentice' to me). But that's when the real fun and games began as the group dynamics were all set up differently. Based upon some earlier team building tasks, some groups were assigned clearly designated leaders whilst other teams were briefed to be more equitable and share leadership responsibilities.

A team of independent judges assessed all the groups and determined that the groups of 'leaders' produced atrocious ideas, followed closely by teams with a single leader. On the flip side, the groups that had balanced the decision-making amongst themselves had developed strategies that scored highly for creativity and with far less internal bickering than the teams with leaders.

The most fascinating facet of their research is that it is counter intuitive and flies in the face of previous studies which have suggested the polar opposite of their findings. However, the belief is that leaders don't necessarily lack the ability to be creative it's just that they work much better on their own rather than in a group. Hildreth explained it like this:

"I think they're looking for verification of their status. There are so many top dogs, maybe that provides uncertainty, and so they want their voice to be heard"

It makes total sense to me given some of the people I have had to e work with over the years. Let's face it, we've all been there at some stage. Brainstorming needs structure and some semblance of a process but what it doesn't need (and all too often gets) is an overbearing, haughty, pompous buffoon who only wants their voice to be heard and their own ideas to be accepted (why am I tempted to put in that picture of Trump again?).

So is being a 'creative' business leader simply a paradox? Well, I'm not so sure. if you take a look at the technology industry we have some extraordinary examples of creative business leaders. Bezos, Jobs and Musk to name but a few. But is their ability to be a creative leader the exception rather than the rule?

Or could it be that this type of creative leader has a single-minded vision, work better in isolation and don't need the consensus of a group to validate their own thinking? Well, if you have seen the Danny Boyle biopic 'Steve Jobs' then that is certainly what Hollywood would have you believe...

As my range of topics started to increase, I began to realise that I should, in turn, expand the disciplines of the groups that I joined and followed.

Consequently, as I wrote about technology I hunted out associated groups. Then it was careers. Then finance. Before I knew it I had filled my quota. There are an awful lot of groups out there that you can join but you do have a limit on the number you can join so choose wisely.

My tactic with groups has been largely consistent. I don't post to these groups on the same day as I publish. I often leave it two days to get some views, likes and comments under my belt and then use this as a hook. For example, in the option to add a headline with your share to the group I would write something like:

10,000+ views. And still rising. Want to know why?

Raising the level of intrigue can have a dramatic effect on the viewing numbers. I have seen them boosted by as much as 10% by this small but highly effective technique.

Frequency of sharing on LinkedIn

One of the initial mistakes I made when I began publishing on LinkedIn was my preconception that once I had launched my article out into the ether then that was all I could do. I hadn't even considered the possibility that I could repost it at a later stage?

I had naively assumed that it was a one-shot deal. And then I started to notice that some of my contemporaries had begun to repost the same articles after a few days or even weeks. I really thought it was a waste of time because surely your contacts / followers will have already seen it. I couldn't have been more wrong.

I decided that I would re-share a piece that I had written about a week earlier. After its initial flood of views it started to recede after a few days and by the time the week had concluded the torrent had slowed to a trickle. Anyway, I decided to give it another try and reposted the same piece. Lo and behold there was an almost instant spike in views aided by a very healthy number of new shares (and even some re-shares from people who had read it previously).

After a bit of thought it all made sense. Not everyone in my community sees my article the first time I publish it. Maybe they were not online or possibly had seen the initial link but were too busy to click on it so it stands to reason that you should try to post more than once.

I have also discovered since that you can even do this with some articles that have been posted several months ago, as long as they are not date sensitive. As I am lucky enough to have a significant increase in followers from month to month it can bring some new content to them and really breathes life into your back catalogue.

Publishing on other Platforms (e.g. trade publications, blogs etc.)

I mentioned much earlier in this book (can you remember that far back?) that I have always written for the trade press in my chosen profession of advertising, media and communications. It has only been since the advent of LinkedIn Publishing and my positive experiences with it that I have switched codes (as it were) and made LinkedIn my primary writing source.

But does that mean you should ignore the trade press? Absolutely not. There can be a symbiotic relationship between the trade press and LinkedIn which is beneficial to both. I have several relationships with a variety of publications around the globe for which I write on a periodical basis. Digital Market Asia, The Internationalist, Mumbrella, Campaign, Marketing, Media Week, Brand Republic, Arabian Marketer and 247 Business are just a few that I have contributed to. Most of the time, as long as there is a tacit agreement between all parties on exclusivity (normally a geographic restriction as opposed to restrictions on a specific platform) then it should be possible to use the same (or at least similar) content across them all.

I spoke to the Chief Editor of Digital Market Asia, Noor Warsia, to garner her opinion. As expected it was typically balanced, honest and forward-thinking:

"It was at the Cannes Lions International Festival of Creativity three years ago when I approached Steve Blakeman to begin penning a regular column for Digital Market Asia (DMA). Being a trade publication that reported on developments which sat at the intersection of marketing and digital/technology is much more difficult than it sounds. For all the sexiness on the subject, not too many of the industry's best focus as much on marketing in a digital world as one would expect.

Steve's daily column, that we had termed as #sowhoknew, instantly proved what every new age editor knows. A well written column from the industry's own will attract more attention than the biggest interviews and the craziest breaking news. Not because these are losing space but because too many platforms today focus on these, and the perception that social media has commoditised news is not very far from the truth. #sowhoknew was our largest read column for every day of the Cannes Lions week, and we insisted on building the relationship with Steve to become a regular weekly columnist with us since. Every Monday, Steve's column was the lead report for DMA since, and for good reason.

Not only did we observe high reader engagement on these columns, with people asking questions to Steve, that he without fail responded to, but they also openly agreed and disagreed with his views. In either case, this was great for us because the best thing a news platform can ask for us is a set of engaged readers, who would tune in especially to read something – appointment reading – if you will. For the unusual instance, when we did not have #sowhoknew in a week, readers enquired about the column. Again, delightful.

There are a few tricks to attract more readers utilising what technology has to offer. A smart 'editorial tech' person keeps an eye out for signs of where articles see more engagement on social platforms. This could include how the author, his own social media circle, his company and its extended social circle share the column, and add to the buzz. The true sense of social 'network' is when it works like a network of one connecting with some and then some with some more and so on. Before you know it, a well articulated thought comes together to become an influencer's weapon in forming mass opinion.

The DMA social media and search team began doing exactly that. #sowhoknew was a permanent fixture *in stories that the team pushed on multiple platforms, across different times of the day to give the column its well deserved boost. The benefit for us? Added readers. Everything has to evolve and grow. Very specifically, in the case of #sowhoknew, we were posed with the all important question – should the editorial policy allow for exclusive write ups which the author, or his company, also wanted to publish on their own blogs (hence non competing platforms) or on professional social networks such as LinkedIn?*

I recall a very long discussion with our senior editorial and tech team on what DMA's take on this should be, when Steve wanted to explore co-publishing on LinkedIn and DMA, at the same time. Given the history of the column on the site, we had decided to go along. And the numbers since indicated that that was a good decision.

Every Monday, before the co-publishing, DMA's readership spiked on an average of 25-27 percent.

When the social and search team put its muscle behind it, this went to 40 percent on a good day (which is very good for a trade publication).

When the co-publishing with LinkedIn began, and Steve Blakeman's column was searched by people beyond what DMA was reaching out to, the column and hence DMA, began attracting newer readership. A dive into Google Analytics indicated that readers from different geographies were reaching the site either through search or our own social push that involved Steve. The reasons for this could vary but it was evident that readers on LinkedIn that began showing interest in the author, were looking for more on what the author had previously written, or any other comments from him.

It was no surprise for us when Steve was named the most influential LinkedIn publisher from our industry for 2015.

While conventional wisdom may dictate that exclusive articles will give the site its best readership, this is one of the many norms that social media has changed. Co-publishing is co-growing in this new age. When seen in the right perspective, it is less competition with social platforms and more collaboration."

I couldn't agree more with Noor. Collaboration is key in this social age and any publication that doesn't realise that fact is going the same way as the dinosaurs. I always try my best to ensure that I cross promote wherever I can (e.g. see the following section on 'Signing Off' for more details) and I only want to work with publications that share the same principle.

By maximising the opportunities to view the article, you also have the potential to make an item go viral. For example, I wrote an item back in March of 2015 about why I believed the humble résumé (or CV if you live in the UK – another example of catering for my largely U.S based audience) was being superseded by having a strong personal profile on LinkedIn (also take a look at the final chapter in this book for my thoughts on that particular topic).

The subject matter was clearly quite punchy (which always helps to accelerate a response) and it did decent traffic on both LinkedIn and Digital Market Asia:

Burn your Résumé - LinkedIn has made it obsolete

(3,934 Views, 111 Likes, 30 Comments)

The famous author Barbara Greene once said "If you tell me, it's an essay. If you show me, it's a story." I wonder if Reid Hoffman, who created LinkedIn, had this notion of storytelling in mind when he was developing the business based social phenomenon. And I have also pondered that as Millennials fully embrace social media for recruitment

purposes, did Hoffman ever envisage that the future success of his idea would effectively consign the humble CV / résumé to the recycling bin?

With 347 million users in over 200 countries, it's fair to say that LinkedIn has become the meeting place for those seeking a new job, wishing to change their current employment or for an employer to find appropriate candidates to fill a vacancy. The reasons for that are complex and varied but maybe it's because LinkedIn has significant advantages over its older sibling. In a nutshell, it's much more three dimensional. It has the capacity to show high quality photographs / videos, can be more easily updated so is more likely to be real time and it shows who you know (and how you are connected) for easy cross reference. Arguably it is also more personal. A résumé isn't necessarily the best way to determine whether a potential employee will be a good social fit for the company. It's too dry and doesn't provide much opportunity to portray your personality, whereas LinkedIn provides more opportunities to demonstrate a little flair.

"Personal branding on LinkedIn is now more important than ever" according to Chris Reed who is CEO at Black Marketing, a global specialist consultancy who focus on enhancing LinkedIn for both individuals and organisations. I asked Chris to expand further and he added "It's not enough to just have a profile, you must bring your personal branding to life on LinkedIn. If you don't then your competitors for that role will. Want that dream marketing role? Make sure you have lots of marketing internships, professional bodies, endorsements and recommendations in your LinkedIn profile."

According to Jaime Klein, founder of Inspire Human Resources, the new Millennial generation most often forget to even bring a paper résumé to an interview. And she has an intriguing take on that as she goes on to say that "can hurt their chances at landing a job. A résumé on nice stock paper shows you have a sense of decorum, especially since the Millennials are being interviewed by Gen X-ers or Boomers." Interestingly though, it is predicted that by 2020 46% of the workforce will be Millennials. So if that's the case then all those X-ers and Boomers will have retired and M-Gens will be taking over those senior roles, thus giving more credence to the argument that obsolescence awaits for the résumé.

Gretchen Gunn a principal at MGD, a staffing firm in New Jersey, is pretty forthright in her view: "Thanks to LinkedIn, I didn't miss a current Wall Street Journal article discussing the death of the paper résumé. So is it true? Is the paper résumé obsolete? Yes. As a staffing partner, I always hand them back to candidates. Why? Because that paper résumé has little chance of leaving my brief case which houses my laptop, iPad, and other electronics. Our entire recruiting process is now online."

It also makes you realize how important it is to ensure that your LinkedIn profile is in good shape. Imagine what messages you are sending out to prospective employers if yours is patchy and incomplete? Does it imply that you are a tech dinosaur who doesn't really understand such things? And if that is the case, does that immediately consign you to the long list of also-rans? As the aforementioned Chris Reed from Black Marketing quite eloquently puts it: "LinkedIn is a 24/7 platform so ensure your profile looks outstanding at all times. LinkedIn never sleeps and neither does your profile."

Echoing and expanding upon that notion, I spoke to talent management 'guru' Chris van Someren (Chief Executive of Ascentador) who offered a typically balanced view: "For me, the key question is not LinkedIn vs a résumé (digital, physical or otherwise) but rather what and how these media communicate about us. Consistency, focus, a well considered point-of-view and accuracy should be the essentials to sharing our career histories no matter in what forum we are presenting them. Our careers need to be present on LinkedIn, of course, and perhaps in other media too (including a traditional résumé) but what we're sharing still trumps where we're sharing it."

So the two Chris's (Van Someren & Reed) make the same valid point. Content is, was and always will be king. It isn't sufficient to simply have what is effectively your CV as your LinkedIn profile. Your job history, skills, endorsements and recommendations are critically important but building your personal professional brand through your social shares is also pivotal. A decent résumé will help you get seen by recruiters, but it doesn't help you get a promotion. Finding a job is one thing but surely more effort should be placed on being better respected in your current job? That's what my good friend Andy Goldman, Global Agency Partner Lead at LinkedIn has said on more than one occasion to me. LinkedIn Members engage with content more than 7x as often as they engage with job properties on the global platform these days. "Being known as a thoughtful, innovative professional through your actions in the workplace is valuable currency for every professional. Publishing lets me share experiences with my teammates, and my clients. It's a cornerstone of social selling which goes way beyond anything a resume could do for us."

And to conclude, a bold statement via a CNN interview with Christina Cacioppo, who is an associate at Union Square Ventures, experts in VC for tech start ups: "A résumé doesn't provide much depth about a candidate. Love it or hate it, social media is your new résumé. Embrace it happily, accept it begrudgingly, outsource it - whatever it takes to keep from getting left behind."

Good news for LinkedIn. And trees.

Bad news for paper manufacturers. And those guys who offer to help you write your résumé for a quick buck.

However, despite the strong response via LinkedIn and Digital Market Asia, one thing I hadn't counted on was that the subject would be picked up by third parties and repurposed into brand new articles. It was only when I received a Google Alert about a week after the initial piece had been posted that I realised that it had been spotted by *Business Insider* and a new article had been fashioned out of my original one:

One CEO says it's time to burn your résumé — here's why

By Kathleen Elkins, Business Insider

By 2020, nearly half of the workforce will be comprised of millennials, according to a report released by the Kenan Flagler Business School.

That means new rules and etiquette will surface in the workplace — particularly when it comes to the way we build our personal brand.

In a recent LinkedIn post, CEO of OMD Asia Pacific Steve Blakeman says traditional paper résumés are becoming obsolete — and explains how the transition to more dynamic social media templates, such as LinkedIn, is underway.

"[LinkedIn is] much more three dimensional. Arguably it is also more personal," writes Blakeman of the professionals networking site that boasts 347 million users in over 200 countries. "A résumé isn't necessarily the best way to determine whether a potential employee will be a good social fit for the company. It's too dry and doesn't provide much opportunity to portray your personality, whereas LinkedIn provides more opportunities to demonstrate a little flair."

In his post, Blakeman included a quote from a CNN interview with Christina Cacioppo, a former associate at Union Square Ventures, which echoes his argument. She told CNN: "A résumé doesn't provide much depth about a candidate. Love it or hate it, social media is your new résumé. Embrace it happily, accept it begrudgingly, outsource it — whatever it takes to keep from getting left behind."

As the glamorous digital résumé takes center stage, it is important not to lose sight of the actual content — your story, experiences, and value — because ultimately, content trumps presentation, warns Chris van Someren, CEO at Ascentador.

Blakeman includes the following quote from van Someren in his LinkedIn post: "For me, the key question is not LinkedIn vs a résumé but rather what and how these media communicate about us. Consistency, focus, a well considered point-of-view and accuracy should be the essentials to sharing our career

histories no matter in what forum we are presenting them."

Don't get left behind, as Cacioppo warns — but don't expect the glitz and glam of a dynamic profile to do all the talking either.

You can only imagine my surprise when I realised that my work had been deemed sufficiently interesting that a journalist had believed the content was good enough to then write their own version.

I immediately set about contacting the journalist, Kathleen Elkins, to see if I could glean any insights into why she had chosen this as a topic to feature. I managed to track her down (using LinkedIn naturally) and it transpires that she had seen the item on LinkedIn initially but had then also read the same piece on Digital Market Asia. This was, if nothing else, further evidence to support cross-platform publishing. Kathleen had also hyperlinked my original article and that in turn had provided another spike in viewing numbers.

She had selected the item because she felt it had something fresh to say and would invite a polarised response (which it did incidentally – I don't think I have _ever_ had so many detractors to anything that I have written). In addition, making that connection has opened up a myriad of additional opportunities most notably a potential new outlet for future features.

And as if that wasn't enough, it didn't quite end there. A couple of days later I received a second Google Alert to inform me that there had been yet another reworked version of the article which had appeared, this time on Yahoo Finance.

And hot on the heels of that variant, there were a slew of country-specific versions including on in The Irish Journal which according to their public online tracker did over 32,000 views alone.

Was that the end of it? Not quite. Almost a year after the original item had been published, I discovered that the article had been quoted in a new book entitled *"Digital Detectives: Solving Information Dilemmas in an Online World"* co-written by Dr Crystal Fulton and Claire McGuinness (available on Amazon).

Fulton and McGuinness are senior lecturers at University College Dublin and their book covers all aspects of social media. In their own words?

"Digital Detectives provides the tools and tactics you need to critically scrutinize web-based digital information to ascertain its authenticity, veracity, and authority."

Here is an excerpt from the book to demonstrate how Fulton and McGuinness interpreted my original article and adapted the content for their own audience:

"In March 2015, Steve Blakeman, the Managing Director of Global Accounts at OMD Worldwide, published an article with an eye-catching title on the business networking site LinkedIn. He exhorted readers to "Burn Your Resume" because "LinkedIn has made it obsolete." Although the headline was designed to be dramatic, Blakeman's reasoning in the article demonstrates just how powerful social media sites and the self-image we project through them have become in the various aspects of our lives.

Blakeman suggests that paper resumes are too 'two-dimensional' to capture the personality and social fit of a prospective employee. A website, such as LinkedIn, "has the capacity to show high quality photographs/videos, can be more easily updated so is more likely to be real time and it shows who you know (and how you are connected) for easy cross reference"

(Blakeman, 2015). He also emphasizes that the professional image that you project through interacting with and publishing on social media sites is essential for advancing in the job you are doing at the moment and for making yourself stand out to current and future employers."

I think it's fair to say that it isn't that easy to make anything you publish on LinkedIn go truly viral. It's hard enough to establish a strong audience on LinkedIn itself without expecting your work to be selected by other publications or book writers. But this example does show what can be achieved and by following some of the advice I have outlined in this and other sections, you will massively improve your chances of viral success.

Signing off

Many of the articles I read from other writers don't have any kind of 'call to action'. Maybe it's because I work in advertising but I almost instinctively seek some kind of reaction from the consumer (or in this case, my reader). It's a good habit to develop because it definitely encourages the reader to actively engage with the piece.

More often than not, I will ask a question related to the subject matter. What follows is a straightforward example of that and it yielded a really strong response especially in terms of comments and shares:

<u>Are you Burned Out or Bored Out?</u>

5,532 Views, 574 Likes, 38 Comments

The classic notion of 'burnout' conjures up mental images of high-flying executives, working insane hours in stressful situations

but being paid top dollar for doing it. However, researchers have discovered that exactly the same symptoms are just as prevalent in more mundane jobs and have named it 'bore-out'.

Being 'bored out' was a term originally coined by Swiss business consultants Philippe Rothlin & Peter Werder in their book 'Diagnose Bore-out'. Essentially being 'bored out' occurs when you are burdened with monotonous tasks on a daily basis. Alternatively, it can also be induced by simply having very little to do. The tedium of relentless routine, whether it be doing nothing at all or repetitive duties, gradually becomes too much to bear for the most individuals and they eventually begin to exhibit the same 3 tell tale signs of burnout:

- physical and emotional exhaustion

- cynicism and social detachment

- feelings of ineffectiveness and lack of accomplishment

Interestingly being 'bored out' is often associated with people who can operate at a highly skilled level but are confronted with a job which offers minimal challenge, thereby resulting in ennui. So if you possess capabilities far beyond what your position entails then you are a prime candidate for 'bore-out'.

Rothlin and Werder also point out that 'bore-out' sufferers are rarely cited as being lazy in the workplace. Paradoxically they have an overwhelming desire to convey the appearance of being busy and can often be observed staring intently at their computer screen whilst informing their colleagues that they are 'super stacked out'.

Does any of this sound familiar? Do you think you might be a victim? As a quick litmus test, you can ask yourself 3 very simple questions:

1. Am I doing my job on automatic pilot?

2. Am I learning anything new?

3. Am I spending too much time on Facebook, LinkedIn, Twitter etc.

If your response pattern is Yes / No / Yes then (although far from being a guaranteed prognosis) you may at least need to consider the possibility that you are headed for 'bore-out'.

So is there any redemption? Well according to veteran psychologist Mihaly Csikszentmihalyi in his book 'The Evolving Self' thankfully there is. He posits that being either 'burned out' or 'bored out' can actually be the springboard for greater wellbeing through personal transformation...

"most novel ideas or behaviours are generated by people who try out new things because they are bored by old routines, or because they are confounded by chaos"

A recent article on Inc.com also offers some practical advice on how to beat the 'bore out'. The main tenet of their argument is that if you allow yourself to stagnate then you will simply accelerate your discouragement. They advocate a focus on 'relentless improvement' by asking yourself 2 questions each and every day:

1. *What is one thing that I want to improve tomorrow?* And it's vital that it is only <u>one</u> improvement as research proves that we are far less effective when we try to do too many things in conjunction

2. *What one thing can I do that could help make the above improvement?* **Try to be as specific as you possibly can and make it an achievable process task that you can readily accomplish. Each tiny step forward puts you on the road to recovery.**

A previous post of mine entitled *Are YOU making yourself unhappy at work?* **covered similar territory and examines how there is very little you can do about life circumstances and absolutely nothing you can do about genetics but you can at least change your outlook on life.**

So have you ever experienced being burned or bored out? And if you have, what exactly did you do to combat it?

The content is thought provoking and (as usual) I tried to add a dash of humour into the proceedings but I think the enquiring nature of the piece, peppered with questions for the reader, definitely helps to encourage interactivity.

So, once you have completed your main feature (and assuming your readers thought your piece was worth reading until the very end) it's always wise to add in a couple of directives or suggestions to your readers.

If they enjoyed reading your work then it makes sense to capitalise on that bonhomie. Come on, there is no point in being a shrinking violet here, you need to take advantage of the situation and hopefully get them to lavish some praise on your masterpiece.

First and foremost, I always thank the reader for simply reading my item in the first place (as we have already established, there is a lot of content out there so the fact that they took the time to read your work over anybody else's is worth applauding).

After showing your gratitude, it's time to ask for something in return. I have my own personal hierarchy of importance when it comes to what they then do with the article. Ideally, what I really want the readers to do is 'share' it. This gives you access to their network of contacts and followers and acts as a real endorsement of the piece (particularly if they add a comment along with that share and tag you as well). It helps to boost the views of your work and as a rough target I always aim for around 5% of my readers to share the item as well. Also, remember to always take the time to 'like' their share and if you have the time try and make a comment too – people seem to respond really well when the author of takes the time to thank them which helps create loyalty amongst your readers and followers.

If you don't get that elusive share? The next best thing is attracting new followers. These guys are really important as they clearly appreciate your work, and want to see more. This means they will become ambassadors for any subsequent work that you put out there. I've always found it difficult to gauge how many new followers you will attract from any one piece that you write. In all fairness, I can't really detect any kind of pattern. I have had items with tens of thousands of views but added only a handful of new followers and yet done much less popular pieces that have yielded a surge of new subscribers.

One rung down from gaining new followers is attracting a comment and I always target around 10% of readers to make statement of some description. Of course, you can't always expect people to be positive about what you have written (as I mentioned on previously) but you have to take the rough with the smooth. And don't forget my previous advice, always take the time to respond 'professionally' to even the most scathing pronouncements.

Finally we come to the humble 'like' which is always great to have but I always wish people had converted their interest into a comment or a share. And if I'm not getting around 15-20% of the viewers 'liking' the article then I always suspect that I must have been doing something wrong!

Of course there are other ways to stir your audience into action such as tweeting, pinning or posting elsewhere (as covered in the earlier section entitled 'Sharing on other Social Platforms). LinkedIn make it easier for some (like Twitter) but don't have handy buttons for all of these options. You should at least suggest to your reader that they consider all of their social feeds to share your work (even though it may be a little more difficult for some of them). And again don't forget, if you have any social activity linked to your work make sure you yourself favourite, like, reshare, retweet etc.

If the content is also available on other publishing platforms (see section on Publishing on Other Platforms) then also make sure that you include those as well (plus hyperlink them). It adds both a level of credibility to the piece because it has been published elsewhere and also helps boost viewing figures by cross promotion.

And whilst we are talking about credibility it's worth highlighting any accolades that you may have earned for your writing. I'm not shy in letting readers know about the awards I received from LinkedIn for 'Top Voices' and 'Agency Publisher of the Year' so if they hadn't spotted that previously on my profile I give them a quick reminder at the end of the piece (suitably tagged so that they can verify it for themselves if necessary).

I will sporadically include a link to another article I have written previously. If there is a connection to the current piece or if I feel it's worth promoting an article that did particularly well then I will add in a link at the end with a note along the lines of *'if you liked this article then you might like this one as well'* - it can really resurrect a previous article that may have gone cold. I have seen some other writers on LinkedIn use this as a sign-off for pretty much all of their work so maybe even I should use it more often.

So what about an example of a typical 'sign off' that I use? Here goes:

THANKS FOR READING - PLEASE FEEL FREE TO FOLLOW, SHARE, COMMENT, LIKE, TWEET, PIN, QUOTE, EMAIL ETC.

THE AUTHOR IS A LINKEDIN TOP 10 WRITER FOR 2015 - 'TOP VOICES' FOR MARKETING & SOCIAL & 'AGENCY PUBLISHER OF THE YEAR'

Also available on: **www.digitalmarket.asia**

If you enjoyed this article maybe try this one from the same author: "Sarcasm= Smarter. Really?"

Naturally you might want to consider something slightly different in terms of the wording and format. As ever, use the basics and then put your own stamp on it.

Re-sharing your work

From time to time, you will write a piece and have fairly lofty aspirations for it. You come up with (what you think) is a fantastic idea for an article, you pore over every detail, you diligently do the research, you carefully craft the story, have someone you trust edit it etc. However, you then unleash it on the LinkedIn masses and it simply fails to ignite.

It's easy to become disillusioned when that happens (and trust me, it will at some stage). You think that what you have written simply hasn't resonated with the audience in the way in which you had hoped and anticipated. You start to chastise yourself that you didn't follow the 'rules of engagement' properly and that's why it failed to connect.

Well, suffice to say that even if you do follow all of the rules in this book it doesn't mean that your work will flourish first time around and it may be worth while revisiting a piece at a later date and trying again.

Now, I don't mean simply re-sharing the original piece, I mean publishing the same item again. Of course, you may want to tweak it slightly if it needs updating or you may want to add in some new research or possibly even spice it up with a better visual. But fundamentally it is the same piece.

To test the theory, I went back through my back catalogue of articles to see if there were any which I felt hadn't done as well as I originally thought. Of course, there were a few. Actually more than a few. But one in particular stood out which was all about why people are too verbose in business and need to talk less and listen more. It was actually one of my first pieces and when I had initially published it the viewing numbers were disappointingly low. It only managed to rack up around 600 views and had no shares at all.

So given that it was almost a year since the original, I decided to see if the same content could elicit a better response, the second time around. I changed very little (added some more tags, changed some images) but it was essentially the same item. And to my surprise (and delight) it did rather well...

Shut Up. Why talking too much can damage your career

(12,665 Views, 1083 Likes, 108 Comments)

"You have two ears and one mouth. You should use them in that ratio". **My old boss, the late (great) Ray Sale often reminded a younger (and considerably more verbose) version of myself of this on a fairly regular basis.**

Ray's sagely advice was brought flooding back to me this week when I saw this picture on LinkedIn...

The WAIT (Why Am I Talking?) mnemonic was remarkably resonant with a considerable

number of LinkedIn users given the high viewing figures, likes and shares I received for the posting. So I decided to do a little more research into the subject to see whether people agree with me that we simply talk too much in business. And I also pondered if being overly garrulous could be detrimental to our careers. What I discovered was actually quite telling...

I'm not sure where the common convention started but it seems to be quite widely accepted that the people who are the most effusive in meetings or on conference calls are considered to be the most influential. Admit it, as a consequence of this unwritten rule we have all been guilty of saying something just so that our voice is heard irrespective of whether we actually had something vital to say. Mea culpa.

So why should it be that talking in business is more revered than listening? Well if you read the research into the matter, it seems that the notion is actually rather superfluous...

In his book 'Just Listen' the author, Dr Mark Goulston, outlines his rather handy Traffic Light Rule. Basically you are on 'green' for the first 20 seconds of anything you have to say. Then you need to watch for the classic signs of boredom from the listener (e.g. fidgeting, looking at their phone, eyes glazing over, snoring etc.). If you don't detect any of these signs then for the next 20 seconds, you are on 'amber' – you can continue but be warned that you are pushing your luck. Beyond 40 seconds? You are on 'red' – so just stop.

The problem though is that most of us have no idea how long 40 seconds actually is when we are gas-bagging. Our ability for time recognition is rendered redundant by the physiological release of dopamine into the brain which provides a natural high and encourages us to continue. Goulston suggests that to combat the urge to be voluble we should practice timing ourselves when talking to ensure that we don't succumb to the desire to filibuster. His basic advice isn't rocket science:

"You need to talk less and listen more"

Part of the problem here is that we are simply predisposed to be chatterboxes. Science says that we humans are social animals and as such are hard wired to use communication as a vital tool to thrive and survive. Now this wouldn't be such a problem, except for the fact that science also tells us that our favourite topic is ourselves. People actually spend around 60% of their time jabbering about themselves (and that figure rises to over 80% on social media). Why? Because of that dopamine rush I mentioned earlier. And it must be a powerful driver - a recent neuroscience study at Harvard University found that individuals were actually willing to pay for the opportunity to disclose information about their lives.

The downside to this propensity to pontificate is that it directly conflicts with our increasingly diminishing attention spans. This phenomenon is caused by the tsunami of information pushed at us each day both verbally and via digital sources. Latest research suggests that our capacity to fully concentrate on what someone else is saying has an upper limit of around 1 minute but can be as low as just 8 seconds.

So what if we ignore all this advice and continue to be a Chatty Cathy or a Blabbing Bob? Well firstly I can't imagine that anyone wants to be labelled in the office as a windbag, oxygen thief or time pirate. Annie Stevens from coaching firm ClearRock, points out that we have little patience for distractions at work, particularly given that 67% of us are working more hours than we were five years ago. Consequently, anyone who is excessively loquacious runs the risk of alienating themselves from their colleagues by impinging upon their precious time. The advice from Stevens is elegantly clear:

"Be brief, be brilliant, and be gone"

Peter Bregman in his article 'If You Want People to Listen, Stop Talking' published in Harvard Business Review, goes one stage further. He extols the virtue of simply saying nothing at all. In his own words:

"Silence is a greatly underestimated source of power. In silence, we can hear not only what is being said, but also what is not being

said. In silence, it can be easier to reach the truth"

Over the years, I have made a concerted effort to take on board some of this advice. But there is a note of caution here as there can be downside... the convention to 'talk more than listen' still appears to prevail in many industries.

I've been quizzed on a few occasions when I haven't uttered much in a meeting or on a conference call. My response is pretty much always the same. *"I'm not talking just for the sake of talking"*. It may not always go down too well as a riposte but at least in my minds eye I can see a little wry smile on the face of a certain Mr Sale...

On reflection, I shouldn't have been that surprised it did so well. At the time it was first posted, I had only been writing for a few months and at that stage I only had a few hundred followers. Also I wasn't really on the radar of the editors ('Top Voices' and 'Agency Publisher of the Year' was a very long way off) so the chances that the piece would be noticed by them was minimal. I also hadn't learned about the best day of the week to publish and also the time zone. In fact, looking back on it now, I knew nothing.

So my advice to you would be this. Don't just 'launch and leave' an article you thought should have done better. Go back to it at some stage in the future and consider giving it another try to see if the spark can turn into a flame.

Grabbing the attention of the Editors

I don't profess to know or understand how the algorithms for aggregating all the data for the LinkedIn editors actually work (to be honest I needed spellchecker just to ensure I spelt algorithms correctly).

Of course, employing the tips I have already outlined in this book will certainly help you get noticed. And there is no substitute for superb content. But none of these can categorically determine whether your work will be featured.

What I can tell you is that those annoying algorithms do their best to curate the editorial items that are likely to have the most traction. Being noticed and featured previously for example gives you a far better chance of your work being picked again (which is great if that has happened but not quite so good if it's your first attempt). Equally, the number of views you have on your article is important but the algorithms seemingly attribute far more significance to higher levels of engagement (e.g. shares, likes and comments). That's why I talked specifically in the previous section on 'Signing Off' about encouraging your readers to go that one step further and push your content out to others and follow you for future articles.

The LinkedIn editors don't really give much insight into what they are looking for but if you dig deep enough there are some clues buried deep along the way that I have unearthed for you.

You might want to take a look at LinkedIn's very own editorial calendar for a list of themes that the editors themselves are seeking to focus on. Each month is dedicated to a different topic such as 'My Big Break' or 'Best Day at Work' or even 'The One Question I Always Get Asked'. They recommend using some of the usual tricks such as links, hashtags and embedded slideshares. So take their advice and do as they ask as it might make all the difference.

Furthermore, the Pulse team actively encourage you to tell them about what you have written and invite writers to let them know about their work. To be honest, I have never tried this method but I know of people who have and they insist it has worked for them.

To tell LinkedIn Pulse team about your post all you have to do is notify them via a tweet with the link of your post, add tip@LinkedInPulse plus a brief description of the content. That's it and if they deem it worthy then it will be chosen.

5. Insights from other successful writers on LinkedIn

After I had completed my personal journey through everything I had learned from publishing on LinkedIn, it occurred to me that I hadn't necessarily found the font of all knowledge when it comes to being a Top 10 Writer; my tips are, of course, subjective. There are, of course, several others who have achieved exactly the same and I thought it would be really interesting for me (the writer of this book) and you (the reader of it) to take a look at how some others achieved the same goal.

I reached out to the 2015 alumni of 'Top Voices' and the 'Agency Publisher of the Year' to see if they could provide validation for my own opinions or even if they could add a completely unique perspective or different dimension? No stone left unturned.

I am thrilled to say that four of those writers agreed to participate in the making of this book and divulge their own hints and tips.

The simple question I posed to each of these writers was as follows:

"What is the main tip you would offer to anyone aspiring to be a Top 10 Writer on LinkedIn and can you provide an example of your work that typifies that very same tip?"

The responses I received from each of them were fascinating in a multitude of ways. It was great to see that they shared some of my thoughts but I was thrilled to see that they also had so much more to add.

Plus, reading their work again made me feel very humble to be associated with such talented writers (yeah, I know that sounds sycophantic and you want someone to pass the bucket but read their work on the following pages and then tell me I was wrong).

Oh and given some of their viewing numbers it occurred to me that maybe they should have written this book and not me. Thank goodness I thought of it before they did...

Marianne Griebler – LinkedIn 'Top Voice'

Marketing Communications Consultant

Marianne Griebler Consulting

Chicago, USA

My top tip? Find the "sweet spot" between your professional expertise and a trending topic that you're passionate about.

Just weeks before the VW scandal broke in fall of 2015, we had friends over for brunch who were proud to show us their new VW Golf diesel. These are thoughtful, intelligent people who did their research before making their purchase (and buying a car is a sizable investment of time and money for most Americans). One thing that really drove their decision was that the Golf promised the "sweet spot between performance and clean energy;" a car that was fun to drive AND had a small carbon footprint. It was irresistible.

And, as we now know, too good to be true.

As the story about VW's duplicity began to unfold, I could not get the faces of my friends out of my mind. Because brands often become an extension of who we are, and the values we cherish, they, like many VW buyers felt betrayed by what happened. I did research to make sure my points were based in fact, but it was my anger at how VW had abused its customers' trust that, literally, fueled the post. They had trashed one of the top brands in the world in pursuit of a better bottom line in the U.S. market.

In other words, write about what you care about. Have a point of view and some passion for your topic and then examine it through the lens of your professional expertise. The very helpful editors at LinkedIn have made it clear that they are not looking for "tips and tricks" posts; they want insights and energy that will spark conversation. Topical posts are especially useful because they tap into the emotions your reader may already be experiencing, and that is a useful tool for encouraging people to comment and share.

I'm not saying you have to be fueled by anger, as I was when I wrote that post. Humor; delight, even joy; curiosity; anything that suggests you have a pulse, a perspective and some enthusiasm makes it easier for your reader to engage too.

Has Volkswagen Smashed Its Brand Promise Beyond Repair?

(210,319 views, 949 Likes, 1002 Comments)

To car buyers looking for the sweet spot between performance and clean energy, Volkswagen's diesel line almost seemed too good to be true.

And sadly, it was.

The dirty footprint of the Volkswagen diesel scandal got even bigger on Tuesday when the company confessed that 11 million vehicles worldwide are equipped with the now-notorious software used to cheat the EPA. And their customers.

At the heart of the issue for many Volkswagen buyers (outside from the lying and the cheating and the fraud) was that they'd been duped into believing they could have their green cake and eat it too.

Clearly, Volkswagen felt driven (pun intended) to take extreme measures to create a product with the right balance between fun and responsibility. The goal? Get ratings to keep the American government off their back while pursuing a coveted market share that had been eluding them.

Delivering on the promise of these vehicles never seemed to be on the table.

This is a sad tumble for the company that was named one of the top global brands in 2014 (praised for being "clear and consistent in its design and brand story") and also awarded the National Energy Globe Award Germany the same year.

But it's not enough to tell a good story. You have to make it real for your customers.

And that's why Volkswagen hasn't just put a few dings in their brand; they may have totalled it.

All of this is fascinating given that only few months ago, Volkswagen listed its intangible assets (which includes goodwill) at $67 billion.

"Volkswagen's goodwill makes up a much larger percentage of its net worth than is the case at other car companies," reports Stephen Gandel of Forbes. "Volkswagen's goodwill and other intangibles makes up about 16% of its total assets. Compare that to just 4% at Daimler and 3% at GM."

Apparently, arrogance takes up a substantial percentage of those intangibles. And it makes perfect sense when you look more closely at where the company's values seem to lie.

Their latest international tagline, "Das Auto" ("The Car"), strikes me as internally, not externally, focused. There's nothing in those two words about the benefit to the customer, about the driving experience they can expect or about how Volkswagen will stand behind their products.

That's a pretty big shift from "the People's Car."

Brand promises are not naive or idealistic. They are actually excellent road maps to success. The right ones are grounded in the knowledge of how a company can make money and thrive by selling benefits that can be consistently delivered.

It's that easy, and that hard.

I can't help but feel a bit sad about how badly Volkswagen has driven off the road. One of my first cars was a very elderly VW Bug that lacked a solid floor but could always be counted on to start on even the frostiest mornings.

Unfortunately, their lame apology is not a good start. (One of the worst, frankly, if that's a point of pride for them.)

I hope they go back to the drawing board to rethink their promise to their customers. I hope they'll make substantial, and expensive, acts of contrition. We will all be watching closely to see how well the repairs go.

Tai Tran – LinkedIn 'Top Voice' & Forbes '30 under 30'

Student & Intern

San Francisco, USA

Be authentic. Successful thought leaders allow their voice and authenticity to exude in their writing. Anyone can write about a given topic or event, but only you can write it with your perspective. This perspective is an accumulation of upbringing, life experiences, and education that makes your voice unique.

#RaceTogether: 3 Reasons Behind Starbucks' Failure

(440,548 Views, 1,273 Likes, 1,132 Comments)

This past week, Starbucks' baristas across 12,000 U.S. stores began writing "Race

Together" on all of its coffee cups. Why? Starbucks wanted to initiate conversations of race and diversity with their customers.

The results? A huge backlash on social media resulting in the temporary closing of Starbucks Sr. VP of Global Communications Corey duBrowa's Twitter account. The intention behind #RaceTogether was noble, but the execution left a lot to be desired. From a marketing perspective, #RaceTogether failed because of (1) poor brand alignment, (2) authenticity deficit, and (3) poor reaction.

Brand Misalignment

Starbucks as a brand has never been associated with racial diversity. Instead, it has been known for premium pricing and even gentrification in some cities. A campaign on race relations and income disparity was quite ironic for a brand such as Starbucks. The nature of #RaceTogether did not align with Starbucks' corporate branding, thus was quickly met with disapproval from customers on the social sphere.

A Tweet Criticizing Starbucks Lack of Corporate Diversity

A Tweet Criticizing #RaceTogether Lack of Diversity

<u>Authenticity Deficit</u>

As a nationwide marketing initiative on race and diversity, Starbucks failed to recognize that their partners, Starbucks version of employees, were not trained to facilitate these types of conversations with customers. Were Starbucks' partners informed enough or even comfortable to discuss on topics of race and diversity with customers?

The overall campaign put partners and customers in an awkward position.

#RaceTogether forced an artificial agenda from corporate Starbucks rather than letting conversations sprout organically. The lack of authenticity caused many customers to feel that Starbucks was misinformed while attempting to cash in on a recent trend. A big no-no for marketing.

Poor Reaction

Any marketer would question whether Starbucks actually had a crisis management plan for #RaceTogether. Social media is a double-edged sword. It could be rewarding yet volatile and unforgiving at the same time. Immediately after the launch of #RaceTogether on March 17, Starbucks customers began flooding social media with their frustrations about the campaign.

Starbucks' response? Not much. Some customers attempted to tweet to Corey duBrowa's Twitter handle to no avail. Shortly, on the same day of #RaceTogether launch, duBrowa's Twitter was deactivated. This further fueled customers' anger with Starbucks—their lack of responsibility and responsiveness. DuBrowa's Twitter handle has since been reactivated.

User Being Blocked by Corey deBrowa's Twitter Handle

Key Takeaways from #RaceTogether for Brands

- **Alignment between your brand perception and everything else you do MUST be present at all time. When a brand becomes out of touch with its own brand perception and customers, another #RaceTogether failure will likely ensue.**

- Authenticity is the driving factor behind any successful marketing campaign. People engage with campaigns, not companies. When there is a disconnect in authenticity, people will feel cheated and react negatively.

- Proactive and reactive thinking should be the number one goal in any campaign development process. Developing and having a plan to react with backlash, whether mild or extreme, prevents a campaign failure from escalating to a point of no return.

Final Thoughts

Despite all the negative criticisms, I firmly believe Starbucks had good intention behind #RaceTogether. The campaign did stir up debates of race and diversity—perhaps not the way Starbucks would have wanted, but it ultimately created buzz over this topic. Starbucks still has the potential to lead this conversation. Let's hope that future campaigns will be developed and executed with the customers in mind.

What are your thoughts about #RaceTogether? What would you have done differently if you were Starbucks? Comment below.

Tai is currently a business undergraduate at UC Berkeley. He is ready to disrupt the tech industry with his infectious passion and energy for marketing! Learn more about his marketing and networking course at the Haas School of Business.

Anthony J James - LinkedIn 'Agency Publisher of the Year' APAC

Managing Director & Chief Innovation Officer

Trinity Consulting Services - Marketing and Advertising

Sydney, Australia

These days, agency professionals have plenty of places to publish. We can write our own blogs, publish to our agency websites, use Facebook Notes, create podcasts and even create videos on platforms like Blab. But it's never just about pushing out content – it's about engaging with our audiences without friction. It's about delivering value. And this is where LinkedIn proves its value.

Amazing things can happen when you use LinkedIn as a publishing platform. It makes you wonder. What more can happen? Who can you reach through the

LinkedIn platform? What kind of impact can you have? And who can you inspire? Make it a resolution to start publishing. Build your professional and personal brand. Be genuine. Share your insight and experience. It's a wide world full of opportunity – and it all starts with a sharing a few words. Get writing!

How to Prevent Innovation From Being Just Plain Boring

You see it every day. Brands talking about how innovative they are, how this new widget will transform their business, and how millions of consumers will run to the nearest store and buy, buy, buy! But if you look a little closer at many of the brands, the new widget is actually just a new bit of coloured plastic, a dodgy phone app, or a brand tie-up with a film or a tourism experience. It may be a new way of doing things (for the brand), but I wouldn't

call it innovation (see my previous post on definition of innovation).

I believe innovation is more about business solutions:

"Deeply understanding the business problem clients face, and then applying properly practiced creativity, a little rule breaking, and collaboration, to delivery solutions that solve the problem, have a positive impact on the brand and drives real growth."

Unfortunately, much 'so called' innovation is just gimmicky or a dull attempt to attract attention. It hasn't changed the firm, or the interaction between a business and its customers. And if it doesn't change things, frankly, what's the point.

In my role, I am keen to ensure that innovation is central to our business, and that we are always innovating in the true sense of the word. But that doesn't mean I think that just any kind of innovation is mandatory for ourselves, or indeed, for the firms we assist. Innovation should be transformative and build new connections. Innovation is inspiring and exciting when it helps change the way a business operates, and when both companies and their customers get more from the exchanges. It helps build productivity, and it makes companies great to work with. Most importantly, innovation should lead to growth.

Surrounded by ideas everyday, I came up with a short questionnaire to help test if it is a truly innovative concept. I use it as a basic tool, a litmus test, to provide guidance.

THE BUILD IT OR BURY IT CONCEPT TEST

1. Does the concept change the way your firm makes its products/does business?

2. Does it change the way you communicate with customers?

3. Is it tapping in to talent and ideas normally outside the firm?

4. Is it giving customers more choice?

5. Does it respond to changes in consumer/business behaviour?

6. Is the value of the innovation easy to understand (even if it is a technically complex solution)?

7. Will its development inspire story-telling?

8. Is it genuinely new, and not just a new costume for old products and practice?

9. Are you getting people calling you up to see how they can get in on the project?

... and finally...

10. Are you SO EXCITED about your innovation that you want to spend all your spare time thinking about it?

If your concepts all get YES responses to these questions, then congratulations, YOU HAVE A COOL INNOVATION. Actually I want to know about it, and to buy it. If you get a YES to more than seven questions, then you may still have a good set of ideas, and we should talk more about how we can make it even more exciting. If you get a YES to only five questions, you probably need to go back and think about how you can generate more change - to markets, to your business, and probably to your agency! But if you got a YES to less than five questions, then think seriously, pivot, apply your learning, or move on!

What do you think of my test? How do your own innovations stand up to it? Should I add any further criteria? Share your thoughts with me in comments, below!

Elie Khouri – LinkedIn 'Agency Publisher of the Year' EMEA

CEO, Omnicom Media Group MENA

Dubai, UAE

What's the most valuable tip I can give someone trying to write a blog post on LinkedIn? It's simple: before you write, take some time to listen to the conversations happening around you.

I like to think of publishing long-form blog posts on LinkedIn as a virtual extension of the conversations I have with my peers, employees, clients and members of the press. It might seem counterintuitive, but in order to speak or write really well, you need to know how to listen.

Before you decide on writing a blogpost, spend some time taking the pulse of your readers. What are they interested in or what could they be interested in?

Taking that in to consideration is essential to creating a meaningful dialogue with your readers. Sometimes adding a slightly controversial slant to a topic of interest can work wonders. For example, consider a LinkedIn post I wrote last year titled "Was Jennifer Anniston the right choice for Emirates?"

The topic was on-trend, slightly controversial and it generated a fantastic debate within LinkedIn and beyond. On LinkedIn, it sparked a whirlwind of 60+ solid comments with several people commenting more than once as the debate roared on. Perhaps even more notably, were the exchanges that particular blog inspired beyond LinkedIn. Employees, peers, clients and the like across the region approached me to give me their two cents on the debate. It truly was a pleasure to see how a very simple blog was getting people to think critically about branding and indeed the purpose of marketing.

At the end of the day, this is the ultimate responsibility of a thought leader: you need to be able to ask the tough or unusual questions to get people to challenge the status quo. Whether you write about marketing, finance, science, mentorship or sustainability, a thought-provoking post has the power to change a fundamental concept, a mindset or even an entire industry. Merely stating your opinion won't empower you to harness that power – so what will?

Unfortunately, there isn't a one-size-fits-all answer to that question. My advice? Always approach blogging the same way you approach conversations. Spend some time actively listening to what people are talking about or commenting on before you settle on a topic. Then carefully reflect on what your opinion on the matter is and what kind of a change you'd like to inspire through your blog.

When I think about writing for LinkedIn, no matter what the subject matter may be, I always have the same intention. I ask myself, will this topic get people thinking and talking? Is it meaty enough to provoke an intelligent conversation? Will it capture the ever-fleeting interest of the average reader on LinkedIn? If I've answered yes to at least two of these questions, I know I'm on to something and you probably will too.

Was Jennifer Aniston the right choice for Emirates?

(4,358 Views, 113 Likes, 68 Comments)

Less than six months after Etihad introduced Hollywood star Nicole Kidman as its brand ambassador, FRIENDS star Jennifer Aniston signed a $5 million global brand endorsement deal with Emirates. Last week the airline announced it will be spending approximately $20 million to run advertisements featuring the actress. That's a lot of money and effort. Will it be worth it? I'm going to reserve my judgment until the campaign is released. Until then, here are my first impressions of the association.

Game of copycat: Regardless of when negotiations really began, announcing Aniston mere months after Kidman, will strike the onlooker as an attempt at catching-up. Emirates has worked long and hard to establish itself as a serious international player in the industry - should it really be playing second fiddle to its much younger and less established Middle Eastern aviation brother? That being said, the onus now lies in the hands of Emirates: will they choose to do something bigger, bolder and better than its counterpart? Will Aniston be seen sitting rigidly in first or business class with a forced smile? Or will we see something so bold and universal, it has the potential to go viral. Cultural relevance: Emirates is a global brand with Middle Eastern roots - a brand ambassador should ideally reflect that rich cultural mix. Compared to other celebrities, America's sweetheart Aniston may be more conservative and controversy-free but some may question her link to the Middle East. Perhaps partnering with a celebrity like Amal Clooney, Salma Hayek or Shakira could help the airline appeal to the star struck while still maintaining a connection to the region. Also, it is worth asking: is Jennifer Aniston's brand big enough for a global company like Emirates? The brands she's been associated with in the past, Smartwater and Aveeno skincare products, pale in comparison to the scale of Emirates. Still, this could be seen as a positive thing when compared to Kidman's multiple partnerships with mega brands like Omega, Chanel and Jimmy Choo which dilutes the power of her endorsement.

Building on brand values: Aniston's charm lies in her girl-next-door persona. While few can doubt her allure, how does it compare to Emirates' bold and daring ethos of Hello Tomorrow? The airline has worked tirelessly to associate itself with exotic destinations, wanderlust and unceasing thirst for adventure. Will Aniston's goofy, down-to-earth persona match up? That being said, perhaps this association is part of a larger initiative to continue building on the association between Emirates and Dubai by tapping into the emirate's values of accessibility, fun and friendliness. Unlike its past sports-heavy ambassadors like Pele and Ronaldo, choosing a household name like Jennifer Aniston could help broaden the airline's appeal and position Dubai as the ultimate tourist destination.

No matter which way you cut it, we are all very excited to see how this will unfold. Until then, let me know what you think of the deal in the comments section down below. Are you with Team Jen? If not, were it up to you who would you rather partner with?

As you can see, there is a common thread running throughout all the excellent advice on display here. Authenticity is certainly key.

I think that is best epitomised by Tai Tran. Not only does his work demonstrate maturity far beyond his years but it also proves that you don't have to be an industry icon to be a successful writer on LinkedIn. It belies the excuse I often hear – nobody will read anything I write because no-one knows who I am or I'm simply not important enough. Well, if an undergraduate like Tai can establish such a huge following on the back of his exceptional writing then you really don't have an excuse do you?

And as you read through the four articles featured here, you can clearly see the differing styles adopted by each of these talented writers. And that again demonstrates to me that there are audiences out there keen to accept and assimilate diverse approaches.

I'm also delighted to see many of the hints, tips and insights I have outlined in this book on display in their writing. Whether it be the use of the listicle, the skill of incorporating a well chosen question or a clever sign-off demanding some type of call to action, it's encouraging to see that these successful writers have also managed to figure out what works.

6. Building Your Personal Brand on LinkedIn

Now we have covered the basics on how to write effectively on LinkedIn and maximise the engagement of your musings, it's now the time to tell you that even if you do all these things if you have not taken account of your personal branding on LinkedIn then much of this advice will be like seed on stony ground.

I have mentioned Chris J Reed (CEO of Black Marketing) a number of times within these pages. And there is a reason for that. He is an expert in personal branding on the medium. He has over 43,000 followers on LinkedIn, has an official LinkedIn Power Profile and a purple Mohican. I think it's fair to say he knows a little bit about the subject of personal branding.

His initial advice is to Google yourself (come on we've all done it). What comes up first? Most likely your LinkedIn profile right? So that is your initial interface with the outside World. And then ask yourself another question: how professional does my profile look? Is it up to date? Am I sharing appropriate information?

Now, I don't want to go off-piste and turn this book into something that it was never intended to be (i.e. a book about how you build a great profile on LinkedIn). There are a plenty of excellent books out there explaining how you do just that and also some very interesting writers publishing about the topic on LinkedIn (funnily enough). That said I believe it is worth covering some of the basics because it is a key component in helping you become a Top 10 Writer. The simple truth is that if you have a weak profile, then your chances of achieving that goal are significantly impaired.

Think carefully about your profile picture. The worst mistake is having no picture at all. It makes people think it's a fake profile, so there is no way people will connect with you or follow you if that's the case. Also, this is not Facebook so don't use a photo that you took on a night out with your pals wearing a luminous green wig and matching mankini. The same goes for a stupid selfie (and definitely not one done in front of a mirror). Don't use a picture of a celebrity. You are not Adele or George Clooney (yes, I have seen examples of both) so don't pretend that you are because people will assume that you are:

a) mad

b) a stalker

c) have delusions of grandeur

d) all the above

Just get a decent picture of yourself taken by a friend or colleague. If you must do a selfie then use your common sense and ensure it isn't taken in your bathroom / bedroom / garden shed etc.

Your profile name should be for just that. Resist the temptation to add your email address, phone number, date of birth, place of birth, weight at birth etc. It isn't necessary and just makes your profile look confusing and makes you appear desperate.

Clean up your LinkedIn public profile URL. The one you have been allocated is not cool and makes you look like a dork:

http://linkedin.com/aaa/billy-hasnoclue23456-hwhwndjr

Just tidy it up by getting rid of the extraneous letters and numbers, just leaving your name. Oh and don't forget to use it in your signature sign-offs. The extra traffic might make all the difference.

Get recommended. Use your network and aim to have at least 10 recommendations from your contacts (and at least one from every position you have held). Ask the people writing about you to make it a little more interesting than "I really liked working with you" which does neither you nor the person who write it any favours whatsoever. To encourage people to write you a recommendation why don't you volunteer to write them one first, then simply request them to reciprocate?

Update your profile on a regular basis. Ensure that all your details are up-to-date, add in any accolades that you have been awarded, features that you have been in, mentions in trade publications etc. All this information adds credibility to you as a writer and encourages people to follow you.

Now, this is a controversial one but, I would encourage you to accept most of the invites that you receive on LinkedIn. Obviously be cautious with the ones that are quite obviously spammers (no picture, very few connections etc.). You will make the odd mistake (less than 5% in my experience) but at least 95% + are genuine. You may also be surprised where some of these conversations can take you. For example, my next book will be a collaboration with another author who read one of my items on LinkedIn, we connected, struck up a bond and that has led to a co-authoring opportunity. In my opinion, that connection alone is worth having to deal with the occasional error when I do get spammed.

I also spoke to David Petherick at Amazes.me who is an industry expert on making you visible, legible & credible on LinkedIn. Interestingly he concurred with all the tips outlined in this section but he also added a few additional ones too:

"Give away useful information. Case studies, tips and advice, practical guides, using PDFs, videos, audio, downloads. The key here is to add value - not to sell.

Share useful information created by others. Monitor the social sphere, blogs and more for information in your area of expertise that adds value, and share it, generously, with your thoughts and interpretation. Don't share maths quizzes or inspirational quotes.

Add comments to stories and discussions to relevant Groups on LinkedIn, and when those in your network share useful information. Be generous and kind, and don't be tempted to sell. You should aim to demonstrate your knowledge with quiet authority.

Set a target of finding, say, two new connections every time you use LinkedIn. You can find them using advanced searches, in groups, from comments they have added, and in the suggestions LinkedIn® provides you from time to time. Send them each a simple, personalised invitation to connect. If you add two a day, you will have over 60 new contacts every month, 700 in a year."

Some people have asked me why personal branding is so important if you only want to write on LinkedIn. My answer is always the same. It's part of the package. Readers want to know about who they are going to follow, where they have worked, what they have done, what have they achieved and why they succeeded. It's further validation of their choice to follow you rather than someone else. Take a look at some of the LinkedIn Influencers if you don't believe me.

A strong example is that of Dr Travis Bradbury. You may not have heard from him previously (only a year ago, I hadn't either). I am a follower of his on LinkedIn (along with a further 637,571 others). He is also an author of a best selling book called Emotional Intelligence 2.0, CEO of TalentSmart and regularly writes for the likes of Newsweek, the New York Times and the Wall Street Journal. Not only that, he finds time to publish on LinkedIn with incredible regularity (at least once a week) and his posts regularly top 200,000+ views. Impressive right?

His personal brand is exceptionally strong and has become a beacon for someone like me who is just embarking on a journey from being a blogger into becoming a published author. And I am well aware that without a serious focus on my own personal brand that is unlikely to happen.

Still unconvinced? Have a quick read of one of the articles I wrote about the subject in November 2015:

Personal branding on LinkedIn a waste of time? 5 myths debunked!

(3,120 Views, 307 Likes, 55 Comments)

"Personal branding? It's a waste of time. I'm too busy working". **Actually that's not my opinion but that of an ex-colleague of mine. Who is currently unemployed. Go figure. Seriously though, anyone who doubts the importance and value of a powerful personal profile on social channels like LinkedIn must be deluded. Or as Gary Vaynerchuck, expert social commentator states:**

"It's important to build a personal brand because it's the only thing you're going to have. Your reputation online, and in the new business world is pretty much the game"

The notion of personal branding has been around for some time. As Oscar Wilde put it so eloquently *"be yourself, everyone else is already taken"*. So why is that some people have such an issue with it? I've taken a look at the top 5 reasons why people are so cynical about developing their own personal brand and debunk some of myths surrounding those barriers...

Myth #1. Personal branding is only for extroverts - or as someone once said to me, it's just bragging. Rubbish. As Muhammad Ali was famously quoted *"it ain't bragging if it's true"*. That said, it is a common misconception that personal branding is really just for gregarious types. The truth is that showing some humility is a distinct advantage when developing your own brand. Authenticity is absolutely key as any savvy employer will easily sniff out any BS. As

William Arruda in his article for Forbes puts it:

"If your approach to personal branding involves wearing a mask... you will fail"

Myth #2. LinkedIn is just like Facebook - The two platforms are entirely distinct and should never be confused (although the lines of demarcation can occasionally be blurred). As Chris J Reed, Global CEO at specialist LinkedIn agency Black Marketing puts it:

"LinkedIn is a peer to peer network in a business context. It's like a business networking event. So whatever you do in a business networking event you should do on LinkedIn"

So, no matter how funny that clip of cats being scared by cucumbers is (that is a thing by the way) just don't share it on LinkedIn. Like I just did. Doh.

Also it's probably a good idea to have a different profile picture on each platform as well. A decent picture of you can increase your profile views by 14x according to LinkedIn. So whilst a shot of you chomping on a mezcal worm whilst ligging out in Cabo may garner some interest it's probably not the best first impression for a prospective employer.

Myth #3. Your personal brand is at odds with the brand of your employer -Your personal branding should actually support corporate branding. Most enlightened employers will empower their employees to express themselves. The only caveat is that it must adhere to the brand values of the organisation. In other words it is 'applied' personal branding. Again, LinkedIn expert

Chris J Reed hits the proverbial nail on the head:

"By leading from the front you will also encourage all your team to do the same thing and posting their own blogs is a great way of marketing your brand and services directly and indirectly"

Myth #4. Personal branding is just too difficult and time consuming - I hear this excuse all the time. The point here is that you will make time if it's important to you. Just 10 minutes a day makes a huge difference. And the fact is, your personal branding <u>should</u> be important to you. According to an article inThe Huffington Post failing to regularly update your LinkedIn account is a big mistake... Jesse Siegal, MD
at ExecuSearch was quoted as saying:

"Posting to LinkedIn at least once a week is key. One way recruiters gauge someone's level of interest in a field and knowledge of industry trends is through frequency of relevant activity on LinkedIn"

What you read, share, like and comment upon all adds to your personal brand. More importantly any content that you may write on your blog, for a trade magazine and via LinkedIn Publishing is a strong indicator for any company that you share the same values and belief system.

Myth #5. I have a decent résumé / CV so I don't need a personal brand - my opinion is that your personal profile on platforms like LinkedIn actually IS your résumé / CV. Have a read of my previous post 'Burn your Resume - LinkedIn has made it obsolete' which makes that very point.

In that piece (which was picked up by the likes of Yahoo Finance and Business Insider) I make the case for how your personal profile is taking the place of the humble résumé And one quote that still jumps out at me is from a CNN interview with Christina Cacioppo, an associate at Union Square Ventures, experts in VC for tech start ups:

"A résumé doesn't provide much depth about a candidate. Love it or hate it, social media is your new résumé. Embrace it happily, accept it begrudgingly, outsource it - whatever it takes to keep from getting left behind."

So what do you think? Is a powerful online personal branding presence a prerequisite or is it just a pile of pixels?

I think you can probably guess my point of view so I wont labour the point. Suffice to say, if you want to make your writing work for you, then work on your personal profile.

6. That's all I've got... now it's your turn

So there you have it. I have given you everything that was in my locker. I held nothing back. Trust me, there will be no sequel to this book. Not least for the fact that 'How to be a Top 10 Writer on LinkedIn 2 – The Revenge' doesn't really work as a title.

I've tried to make this book as entertaining as possible and put a little bit of a human story into what is essentially a business book. I hope it worked.

If you follow all these rules & tips and carve out a decent personal profile then I believe that anyone on LinkedIn with a rudimentary understanding of language and grammar can have a decent attempt at writing engaging work.

There really is no one simple way of ensuring that your work will be read. The proverbial silver bullet doesn't exist. But by carefully incorporating all the suggestions I have made, or at least a combination of some of them, then you really will give yourself a very strong chance of building a loyal and engaged following. And who knows, maybe you will be one of LinkedIn's 'Top Voices' or 'Agency Publisher of the Year' at some stage too.

I will leave you with another quote from Daniel Roth (Executive Editor at LinkedIn) who was interviewed by Forbes magazine about the rationale for putting together the 'Top Voices' initiative. He puts it most eloquently and I feel it's a fitting way to end:

"Most of these are not professional writers. They have day jobs. But they are developing expertise - these are businesspeople with a corpus of knowledge that you can now share with others along the road. I find this incredibly intriguing. Anyone can write and share and talk about what they know"

So I guess there is only one thing left to say now...

What's stopping you?

Acknowledgements

Many thanks to the various contributors to, and inspiration for, this book:

- Andy Goldman from LinkedIn for encouraging me to write on the LinkedIn Publishing platform in the first place

- Jordan Harries from the Financial Times for her expert editing and proof reading

- Jodi Neuhauser from Maxus for putting me forward for 'Agency Publisher of the Year'

- Noor Warsia from Digital Market Asia for unswerving support and for agreeing to test the theory of multi-platform publishing

- Marianne Griebler, LinkedIn Top Voice, for allowing me to feature her work

- Tai Tran, LinkedIn Top Voice for allowing me to feature his work

- Anthony J James, LinkedIn Agency Publisher of the Year for APAC, for allowing me to feature his work

- Elie Khouri, LinkedIn Agency Publisher of the Year for EMEA, for allowing me to feature his work

- Chris J Reed from Black Marketing for his continued support and excellent quotes

- Chris van Someren from Ascentador for being an inspiration and providing unique perspective

- David Petherick from Amazes.me for his valuable insights on personal branding

- Ian Gee, from Geenius Consulting, for his wise words

- Richard Ticehurst for his excellent photography on the front / back covers

- Justine Blakeman, Ella Blakeman, Georgia Blakeman & Alexa Blakeman for being so patient whilst I was locked away writing

- Stephen King, writer. For writing.

57622886R00187

Made in the USA
Charleston, SC
17 June 2016